SEMICOLON

SEMICOLON

How a misunderstood
punctuation mark can improve
your writing, enrich your reading
and even change your life

CECELIA WATSON

4th ESTATE · *London*

4th Estate
An imprint of HarperCollins*Publishers*
1 London Bridge Street
London SE1 9GF

www.4thEstate.co.uk

First published in Great Britain in 2019 by 4th Estate
First published in the United States in 2019 by Ecco,
an imprint of HarperCollins*Publishers*

1

Parts of this book were previously published in *Critical Inquiry*

Illustrations by Anthony Russo
Photo on page 106 © Ralph Crane/The LIFE Images
Collection/Getty Images

A catalogue record for this book is
available from the British Library

ISBN 978-0-00-829153-2

Set in Janson Text with Sofia Pro display
Printed and bound in Great Britain by
CPI Group (UK) Ltd, Croydon

MIX
Paper from
responsible sources
FSC™ C007454

This book is produced from independently certified FSC™ paper
to ensure responsible forest management

For more information visit: www.harpercollins.co.uk/green

For my parents,
who made sure I always had enough to read

Punctuation is a gentle and unobtrusive art that has long been one of the misfortunes of man. For about three hundred years it has been harassing him, and bewildering him with its quiet contrariness, and no amount of usage seems to make him grow in familiarity with the art.

'Power of Points: Punctuation That Upset Work of Solons', *Boston Daily Globe*, 20 January 1901

CONTENTS

VIII

PERSUASION AND PRETENSION

Are Semicolons for Snobs?

Conclusion

AGAINST THE RULES?

LOVE, HATE AND SEMICOLONS

'The semicolon has become so hateful to me,' confessed
Paul Robinson in a *New Republic* essay, 'that I feel almost
morally compromised when I use it.' When Robinson, a
humanities professor at Stanford, sees a dot balanced over
a comma, he's filled with 'exasperation'. Robinson is
perhaps the semicolon's most devoted foe, but he's hardly
its only modern detractor. Novelists from George Orwell
to Donald Barthelme have held forth on its ugliness, or
irrelevance, or both. Kurt Vonnegut advised omitting
them entirely, accusing them of 'representing absolutely
nothing. All they do,' he admonished writers, 'is show
you've been to college.' And almost 800,000 people have

shared a web comic that labels the semicolon 'the most feared punctuation mark on earth'. Yet when the Italian humanists invented the semicolon in the fifteenth century, they conceived of it as an aid to clarity, not (as Professor Robinson now characterises it) a 'pretentious' mark used chiefly to 'gloss over an imprecise thought'. In the late 1800s, the semicolon was downright *trendy*, its frequency of use far outstripping that of one of its relatives, the colon. How did the semicolon, once regarded with admiration, come to seem so offensive, so unwieldy, to so many people?

Asking this question might seem academic in all the worst ways: what practical value could there be in mulling over punctuation, and in particular its history, when we have efficiently slim guidebooks like Strunk and White's *The Elements of Style* and thick reference volumes like *The Oxford Manual of Style* to set straight our misplaced colons and commas? We have *rules* for this sort of thing! But rule-based punctuation guides are a relatively recent invention. Prior to the 1800s, the majority of grammarians and scholars advocated personal taste and judgment as a guide to punctuating, or 'pointing', a text. The Scottish Enlightenment philosopher George Campbell, writing the same year the United States Declaration of Independence was signed, argued that 'language is purely a species of fashion ... It is not the business of grammar, as some critics seem preposterously to imagine, to give law to the fashions which regulate our speech.'

Yet what Campbell and most of his contemporaries thought was a 'preposterous' idea soon became a commonplace principle: as the 1700s drew to a close, new grammar books began to espouse systems of rules that were purportedly derived from logic. In these new books, grammarians didn't hesitate to impugn the grammar of writers traditionally considered superb stylists: Milton and Shakespeare were chastised for 'gross mistakes', and subjected to grammarians' emendations, so that these great authors' works were made to fall in line with rules established centuries after their deaths.

But a strange thing happened as the new genre of grammar rule books developed: instead of making people less confused about grammar, rule books seemed to cause *more* problems. No one knew *which* system of rules was the most correct one, and the more specific the grammarians made their guidelines for using punctuation marks like the semicolon, the more confusing those punctuation marks became. The more defined the function of the semicolon became, the more anxiety people experienced about when to use a semicolon in writing and how to interpret one while reading. Grammarians fought viciously over the supremacy of their individual sets of rules, scorching one another in the nineteenth-century equivalent of flame wars. Courts of law, too, were in a lather over how to deal with punctuation marks: a semicolon in an 1875 legal statute caused all of Boston to fly into a panic when courts opined that it meant that alcohol couldn't be served past 11 p.m. (Bostonians, ever resourceful, devised some pretty clever ways to get drunk well into the wee hours until the statute was finally revised six years after it went into force.)

The story of the semicolon told in these pages follows a chronological path, charting its transformation from a mark designed to create clarity to a mark destined to create confusion. The events described here epitomise the major steps in the life of the semicolon: they show how it was transformed over time, and what was important about those transformations. That importance lies in the semicolon's ability to symbolise and trigger ideas and emotions that transcend the punctuation mark itself. The semicolon is a place where our anxieties and our aspirations about language, class, and education are concentrated, so that in this small mark big ideas are distilled down to a few winking drops of ink.

The semicolon's biography is also a story about grammar and language more generally – and this history will challenge the *myth* most of us like to tell ourselves about grammar. Grammar (in our mythical narrative) is part of the good old days: people used to know grammar *properly*, we think, the same way they used to walk three miles to school uphill in the snow, and everyone was polite and better looking and thin and well dressed. There are reasons why these romantic visions of the past flourish in our collective consciousness: the stories of our grandparents; old black-and-white portraits that freeze the past in Sunday best; and most powerfully of all, a vague shared sense that the world is growing less innocent and less coherent, and that the past must therefore be better the further back uphill into it we are able to climb. Things were harder in some ways back then, we acknowledge; but weren't they also better and purer, too?

'It's tough being a stickler for puntuation these days,' sighs Lynne Truss in *Eats, Shoots & Leaves*, as if before 'these days' there was a time when everyone was committed to proper grammar and everyone agreed on what proper grammar constituted. Self-styled grammar 'sticklers', 'snobs', 'nazis', and 'bitches' want so much to get back to that point in the past where the majority of people respected language and understood its nuances, and society at large shared a common understanding of grammar rules. But that past utopia is a mirage. There was no time when everyone spoke flawless English and people punctuated 'properly'. It's important to come to grips with this historical fact, because it influences how we act in the present: after we nail down some basic punctuation history here through the story of the semicolon, I'll show that hanging on to the old story about grammar – the mythical story – limits our relationship with language. It keeps us from seeing, describing, and creating beauty in language that rules can't comprehend.

I wouldn't deny that there's joy in knowing a set of grammar rules; there is always joy in mastery of some branch of knowledge. But there is much *more* joy in becoming a reader who can understand and explain how it is that a punctuation mark can create meaning in language that goes beyond just delineating the logical structure of a sentence. Great punctuation can create music, paint a picture, or conjure emotions. This book will show you how the semicolon is essential to the effectiveness and aesthetic appeal of passages from Herman Melville, Raymond Chandler, Henry James, Irvine Welsh, Rebecca Solnit, and other masters of English fiction and non-fiction. Looking at these authors, we will see beautiful uses of the semicolon that cannot be adequately encapsulated in grammarians' rules, nor explained simply as a 'breaking' of those rules.

Still, inadequate and artificial as grammar rules are, I understand what it's like to love them. In fact, I'm a reformed grammar fetishist myself, the sort of person who used to feel that her love for English was best expressed by means of irritation at the sight of a misplaced apostrophe, or outright heart palpitations over a comma splice. My own dive into the history of the semicolon was precipitated by a fight over one that my PhD adviser, Bob,* had circled in one of my papers, alleging that it violated the precepts of *The Chicago Manual of Style* (at the time, Bob was chair of the board of the press that publishes the *Manual*). I insisted that the semicolon in question was a perfectly legitimate interpretation of one of the umpteen semicolon rules the *Manual* laid out, and round and round Bob and I went for weeks, grandstanding about the meaning of the *Manual*'s rules. Finally, during one of these heated debates, it occurred to me to wonder: *Where do they come from, these rules I cherish so much, and believe I know so well?*

---

* Robert J. Richards at the University of Chicago. As of 28 March 2018, Bob's entry on Wikipedia contains semicolon usage that I'm quite certain would rankle him: 'Richards earned two PhDs; one in the History of Science from the University of Chicago and another in Philosophy from St Louis University.' Bob, I swear it wasn't me!

Answering that question took me on a ten-year journey through piles of dusty grammar books that had lain
untouched on library shelves for decades, and more often
centuries. Some, having been forgotten for so long,
collapsed in my hands; others left my palms tinted a guilty
red with rot from their decaying leather bindings. But the
words inside those old grammar books had lost none of
their liveliness and passion, and I soon became absorbed
in the drama of grammarians' attempts to create a market
for their rules in the face of an initially sceptical public.
The story that I began to piece together from their pages
called on all my skills as an academic. It demanded my
expertise in the history of science: grammar rules, it turns
out, began as an attempt to 'scientise' language, because
science was what parents wanted their children to be
taught in public [state] schools. Equally, the story of the
semicolon called on my training in philosophy, as I began
to wonder what ethical imperatives knowing the true
history of grammar rules might impose. And finally,
crucial to making sense of the story of the semicolon were
my years of experience teaching writing at institutions like
Yale, the University of Chicago, and Bard College.

By the time I had finished writing the story contained
in these pages, I had changed everything about how I
looked at grammar. I still love language, but I love it in a

richer way. Not only did I become a better and more sensitive reader and a more capable teacher, I also became a better person. Perhaps that sounds like a fancifully hyperbolic claim – can changing our relationship with grammar really make us better human beings? By the end of this book, I hope to persuade you that reconsidering grammar rules will do exactly that, by refocusing us on the deepest, most primary value and purpose of language: true communication and openness to others.

But before I can try to persuade you of this, we have to look the past square in the face. Ever since grammar rules were invented, they have caused at least as much confusion and distress as they have ameliorated; and people living one hundred years ago had passions about semicolons that varied from decade to decade and person to person. In this regard, they aren't so different from us after all: when you looked at the semicolons on the front of this book, you probably felt something. Was it hate, like Paul Robinson? Anger? Love? Curiosity? Confusion? The diminutive semicolon can inspire great passion. As you'll see in the chapters that follow, it always has.

DEEP HISTORY

The Birth of the Semicolon

The semicolon was born in Venice in 1494. It was meant to signify a pause of a length somewhere between that of the comma and that of the colon, and this heritage was reflected in its form, which combines both of those marks. It was born into a time period of writerly experimentation and invention, a time when there were no punctuation rules, and readers created and discarded novel punctuation marks regularly. Texts (both handwritten and printed) record punctuation testing and tinkering by fifteenth-century literati known as the Italian humanists. The humanists put a premium on eloquence and excellence in writing, and they called for the study and retranscription of Greek and Roman classical texts as a way to effect a 'cultural rebirth' after the gloomy Middle Ages. In the service of these two goals, humanists published new writing and revised, repunctuated, and reprinted classical texts.

One of these humanists, Aldus Manutius, was the matchmaker who paired up comma and colon to create the semicolon. Manutius was a printer and publisher, and the first literary Latin text he issued was *De Aetna*, by his contemporary Pietro Bembo. *De Aetna* was an essay, written in dialogue form, about climbing volcanic Mount Etna in Italy. On its pages lay a new hybrid mark, specially cut for this text by Bolognese type designer Francesco Griffo: the semicolon (and Griffo dreamed up a nice plump version) is sprinkled here and there throughout the text, conspiring with colons, commas, and parentheses to aid readers.

In this snippet, you can see four of these brand-new semicolons. You might think you see eight, but beware! That semicolonish mark at the end of the fourth line from the bottom isn't a semicolon, it's an abbreviation for *que*, Latin for 'and'. In this case, it's helping to shorten *neque*, or 'also not'. It appears elsewhere in the excerpt, always filling in the –ue part of a *que*. If you look closely, you'll see that the dot-and-curve combination is raised higher

politani etiam tractus extimantur. Ni-
uibus per hyemem ferè totus mons ca-
net:cacumen neq; per aestatem uiduatur.
B. P. Quid,quod hyemare tantum
eas meminit Strabo? B. F. At experien
tia ita te docet,usq; ipse auctor (quod qui
dem uenia illius dixerim) non deterior.
Quare illud mi páter etiã,atq; etiam uide;
ne quid te moueat,si aliqua ex parte huius
nostri de Aetna sermonis cum uetustis scri
ptoribus dissentimus:nihil enim impedit
fuisse tum ea omnia, quae ipsi olim tradi
dere,quorum permãserint plurima in no
stram diem;quaedam se immutauerit;ali
qua etiam surrexerint noua:nam(ut caete
ra omittam); quod cinerosa partim esse
summa cacumina dictauere;eius rei nunc
uestigium nullú apparet:cinis enim, qui
queat conspici,toto môte nullus est: neq;
id tamen omnibus annis fuit: nam mul
torum testimonio accepimus, qui ui-
dere , annos ab hinc quadraginta tan-

Bembo   Poliphilus   Garamond   Jenson   Palatino   Gill Sans   Didot

up than a semicolon; it's positioned on the same level as the words in the text because it's shorthand for a word instead of a signal to pause.

Nearly as soon as the ink was dry on those first semi-colons, they began to proliferate, and newly cut font families began to include them as a matter of course. The Bembo typeface's tall semicolon was the original that appeared in *De Aetna*, with its comma-half tensely coiled, tail thorn-sharp beneath the perfect orb thrown high above it. The semicolon in Poliphilus, relaxed and fuzzy, looks casual in comparison, like a Keith Haring character taking a break from buzzing. Garamond's semicolon is watchful, aggressive, and elegant, its lower half a cobra's head arced back to strike. Jenson's is a simple shooting star. We moderns have accumulated a host of characterful semicolons to choose from: Palatino's is a thin flapper in a big hat, slouched against the wall at a party. Gill Sans MT's semicolon has perfect posture, while Didot's puffs its chest out pridefully. (For the post-modernist writer Donald Barthelme, none of these punch-cut* disguises could ever conceal the semicolon's innate hideousness: to him it was 'ugly, ugly as a tick on a dog's belly'.)

The semicolon had successfully colonised the letter cases of the best presses in Europe, but other newborn punctuation marks were not so lucky. The humanists tried out a lot of new punctuation ideas, but most of those marks had short lifespans. Some of the printed texts that appeared in the centuries surrounding the semicolon's birth look as though they are written partially in secret code: they are filled with mysterious dots, dashes, swoops, and curlicues. There were marks for the minutest distinctions and the most specific occasions. For instance, there was once a *punctus percontativus*, or rhetorical question mark, which was a mirror-image version of the question mark. Why did the semicolon survive and thrive when other marks did not? Probably because it was *useful*. Readers, writers, and printers found that the semicolon was worth the trouble to insert. The rhetorical question mark, on the other hand, faltered and then fizzled out completely. This isn't too surprising: does anyone really

---

* Back in the humanists' day, the letters for a font were carved into steel bars. These were called 'punches'. The technique was punch-cutting, and its practitioner a punch-cutter.

need a special punctuation mark to know when a question is rhetorical?

In humanist times, just as in our own, hand-wringing sages forecast a literary apocalypse precipitated by too-casual attitudes to punctuation. 'It is not concealed from you how great a shortage there is of intelligent scribes in these times,' wrote one French humanist to another,

> and above all in transcribing those things which observe style to any degree; in which unless points and marks of *distinctions*, by which the style flows through the *cola*, *commata*, and *periodi*, are separated with more attentive diligence, that which is written is confused and barbarous ... Which carelessness, in my opinion, has occurred chiefly since we have for a long time lacked eloquence, in which these things are necessary: the ancient manner of handwriting, therefore, in which the scribes of books (*antiquarii*) were gradually writing a perfect and correctly formed script with precise punctuation (*certa distinctione*) of *clausulae* and with notes of accentuation, has perished together with the art of expression (*dictatu*).

The entire art of expression – dead, because careless writers just couldn't hack it when it came to punctuation. Well, I think we moderns might maintain that the art of expression gave us a few rather decent literary works even after the date of this fifteenth-century letter. But the lament of the French humanists is familiar, isn't it? People can't punctuate correctly, eloquence is slowly dying out. *Plus ça change*.

Still, a few bad-tempered complainants notwithstanding, most humanists believed that each writer should work out his punctuation for himself,* rather than employing a predetermined set of rules. A writer or an annotating reader was to exercise his own taste and judgment. This idea of punctuation as a matter of individual taste and style outlived the humanists: it stretched beyond the Latin texts that Manutius printed, crossing borders and oceans, and it survived as a way of thinking about the practice of punctuation well into the eighteenth century. When the topic of punctuation usage came up, a reader was likely to be advised that he should consider the punctuation marks analogous to rests in music, and deploy them according to the musical effect he wanted to achieve. How on earth did

---

* In those days, it was usually a 'him', although there were of course exceptions.

this idea of the writer as musician, which held on for hundreds of years, transform into our comparatively new expectation that writers must submit to rigid rules?

II

THE SCIENCE OF SEMICOLONS

English Grammar Wars

Goold Brown, an American schoolteacher and grammar obsessive, had a lofty ambition: he wanted to produce 'something like a complete grammar of the English language'. Twenty-seven years after first resolving to undertake this task, he finally published *The Grammar of English Grammars*, which contained 1,192 pages filled with tiny print surveying a selection* of 548 English

---

* I'm surprised he could bring himself to use a selection. Brown was a thorough guy, the type of person who dated his copy of Churchill's *English Grammar* 'AD 1824', lest anyone mistakenly think he might have bought it in 1824 BC.

grammar books that had been published in the eighteenth and nineteenth centuries, up until the 1851 printing of his own book.*

Where were all of these grammar books that Goold Brown surveyed coming from, and what had made them explode in number so suddenly, after several quiet centuries of minimal punctuation guidance for writers? A jaunt through some of the most popular grammar books of the nineteenth century will reveal that their authors were shrewd entrepreneurs taking advantage of a newly developed and highly lucrative market for education in English writing; in both America and Britain, access to public education expanded exponentially over the course of the nineteenth century, and with it, the opportunity to make a killing supplying schools with teaching materials. These early grammarians were also masters of the biting insult, as they jockeyed for position (and market share) with one another. And – perhaps most surprisingly – they were aspiring *scientists*. We have to understand the great shift these authors created in the way people thought about

---

* My copy of Brown's compendium is a menacing leather-bound brick measuring 9¾ inches by 6½ inches by 3 inches and tipping the scales at 4 pounds 15 ounces. It's caused my checked baggage to violate airline weight allowances on three occasions.

English grammar in order to understand the semicolon's transformation: although these first professional grammarians sought clarity through rules, they ended up creating confusion, and the semicolon was collateral damage.

The first English grammar book to achieve lasting influence and popularity by creating laws for language was Robert Lowth's 1758 *A Short Introduction to English Grammar*. Lowth, a bishop in the Church of England and a professor of poetry at Oxford,* used his platform to

---

* Lowth, obviously, was English – unlike Brown, the American meta-grammarian who opened this chapter. I'll bounce back and forth across the Atlantic throughout this chapter, but not without reason. In the nineteenth century, the most influential grammar books enjoyed the same freedom to be bought, taught, and sold on both sides of the pond. This makes a good deal of sense when you think about it: in matters of grammar, differences between British and American English are far slighter than in matters of vocabulary and idiom. In this respect, the distinction between American and British English is analogous to distinctions you'll have encountered within Britain itself: whether you put your bacon on a cob, bap, barm, bun, or roll, you were taught the same grammar rules in primary school as anyone you meet from another region. And that's not the only reason nineteenth-century grammar books were able to slip across borders so easily; frequently the matters on which American and British punctuation have come to differ weren't even mentioned in the books. Peter Bullions, for instance, a New Yorker whose grammar had one of the boldly announce that it was his aim to 'lay down rules' for grammar. These rules, he felt, were usually best presented by showing violations of them along with judicious corrections. Accordingly, he assembled examples from some of the very worst syntactical offenders available in English at the time – true grammatical failures including Shakespeare, Donne, Pope, Swift, and Milton.

Even though Lowth didn't hesitate to perpetrate brow-raising 'corrections' on writers who seem, well, pretty competent, he did still carry with him the legacy of the previous centuries' emphasis on personal taste and style, and he reserved a place for individual discretion, particularly when it came to punctuation. For punctuation, he acknowledged, 'few precise rules can be given,

---

longer sections on punctuation available at the time, doesn't say a word about where punctuation should fall relative to quotation marks. Whether you want your full stops and commas included in (American style) or excluded from (British style) the quotation mark's embrace, you'd find nothing in many of the original grammar rule books to help or hinder you. Even Noah Webster, who advocated fiercely for a uniquely American language befitting a unique new government, didn't distinguish between American and British punctuation styles in his 1822 grammar book. And Robert Lowth, the Englishman we're now discussing, used full stops after abbreviations like 'Mr.', which we now think of as American-style punctuation.

(1) Some Writers have ufed *Ye* as the Objective Cafe Plural of the Pronoun of the Second Perfon; very improperly, and ungrammatically.

" The more fhame for *ye* : holy men I thought *ye*."
Shakfpeare, Hen. VIII.

" But tyrants dread *ye*, left your juft degree
Transfer the pow'r, and fet the people free."
Prior.

" His wrath, which one day will deftroy *ye* both. "
Milton, P. L. ii. 734.

Milton ufes the fame manner of expreffion in a few other places of his Paradife Loft, and more frequently in his

Shakespeare and Milton, both very improper!

which will hold without exception in all cases; but much must be left to the judgment and taste of the writer'. As we've seen before, the marks of punctuation were analogous to the rests in a piece of music, and were to be applied as individual circumstances and preferences dictated. The comma thus was a pause shorter than the semicolon, and the semicolon was a pause shorter than the colon.

Lowth's book reigned supreme in both the UK and the US for a couple of decades, until an American grammarian, Lindley Murray, came along and decided he could probably sell a few books himself if he tweaked Lowth's work a bit by increasing its structural precision and its rigidity. In order to rebuild the book in this way, he divided it into sections and numbered its rules. Murray retitled this new version *English Grammar*. To say that *English Grammar* was a blockbuster success is an understatement.

> " Oft have I feen a timely-parted ghoft,
> Of afhy femblance, meagre, pale, and bloodlefs,
> Being all defcended to the lab'ring heart,
> *Who,* in the conflict that *it* holds with death,
> Attracts the fame for aidance 'gainft the enemy."
>   Shakefpear, 2 Hen. VI.
> It ought to be,
> " *Which,* in the conflict that *it* holds "——
> Or, perhaps more poetically,
> " *Who,* in the conflict that *he* holds with death."

Lowth giving Shakespeare a little lesson in grammar and poetry writing.*

---

* You will notice an odd typographical quirk in Lowth's text: the 'Medial S', which looks to the modern eye like an *f* but is to be read as an *s*. The Medial S can lead to some unintentionally seedy reading in books that are reprinted in facsimile edition, like Antoine Lavoisier's *Elements of Chemistry*, which contains a long section in which the author describes sucking air through a tube for an experiment.

The book went into twenty-four editions, reprinted by sixteen different American publishers between 1797 and 1870, and it sold so many copies that Murray was 'the best-selling producer of books *in the world*' between 1800 and 1840.

Just as Murray found success renovating Lowth's foundations, so Murray's grammar had some additions nailed on by another upstart grammarian, Samuel Kirkham. Kirkham's 1823 grammar gradually displaced its archetype. Where Murray's grammar had gone into a dizzying twenty-four editions, Kirkham's went into at least *one hundred and ten*. Kirkham won over readers by presenting a new system of parsing verbs, and by extending his predecessors' criticisms of 'false syntax' in historical English. Even as Kirkham's book represented a further step towards *more* rules and *more* systematisation, the very first edition of his grammar omitted punctuation entirely, on the grounds that it was part of prosody rather than grammar: in other words, punctuation was all about establishing rhythm, intonation, and stresses. This stance got Kirkham some critical reviews, however; as a consequence, subsequent editions covered punctuation – but only briefly, and only by nebulously describing punctuation marks as pauses of varying lengths. Thus, for the king of nineteenth-century grammar-book sales, punctuation remained a tool that writers could wield with a good bit of flexibility and discretion.

With sales of his book so high, Kirkham was in the spotlight. Not only did that open him up to attack, but it even allowed him to cultivate a proper *nemesis*. That nemesis was Goold Brown, the grammar surveyor in whose gargantuan book Kirkham was but one of hundreds of other people plying the same trade. But out of all those grammarians, Kirkham was the one who most got under Brown's skin. As Brown saw it, Kirkham had played fast and loose with grammar, and cared more about his bottom line than about scientific scruples: he wanted to 'veer his course according to the *trade-wind*', Brown sniped. In Brown's eyes, when Kirkham revised his grammar book to include punctuation, the additions represented not honest scholarly progression but mercenary modifications: 'his whole design' was a 'paltry scheme of present income'. And – Brown added – Kirkham's character was such that he was 'filled with glad wonder at his own popularity'. Labelling Kirkham a quack and a plagiarist, Brown tore into his grammar book on page after page, pointing out its logical contradictions and omissions. Interspersed with these *ad librum* jabs are some choice *ad hominem* sucker punches. In one particularly efficient passage, Brown calls out Kirkham's reasoning while also claiming that he didn't write his own book *and* insinuating that he was too cheap to pay his ghostwriter adequately:

As a grammarian, Kirkham claims to be second only to Lindley Murray; and says, 'Since the days of Lowth, no other work on grammar, Murray's only excepted, has been so favorably received by the *publick* as his own. As a proof of this, he would mention, that within the last six years it has passed through *fifty* editions.' – *Preface to Elocution*, p. 12. And, at the same time, and in the same preface, he complains, that, 'Of all the labors done under the sun, the labors *of the pen* meet with the poorest reward.' – *Ibid.*, p. 5. This too clearly favours the report, that his books were not written by himself, but by others whom he hired. Possibly, the anonymous helper may here have penned, not his employer's feeling, but a line of his own experience. But I choose to ascribe the passage to the professed author, and to hold him answerable for the inconsistency.

Kirkham answered Brown's complaints about his boasting with … more boasting, this time underlined with populist rhetoric aimed at his American readers:

> What! A book have no merit, and yet be called for at the rate of *sixty thousand copies a year*! What a slander is this upon the public taste! What an insult to the understanding and discrimination of the good people of these United States! According to this reasoning, all the inhabitants of our land must be fools, except one man, and that man is GOOLD BROWN!

Brown bit back, pointing out that Lord Byron got paid a lot more for *Childe Harold* than Milton did for *Paradise Lost*; but would anyone say *Byron* was the greater literary genius?

Brown and Kirkham may have pitted themselves against one another,* but they (along with their contemporaries) agreed on one thing: grammar was to be viewed

---

* When Brown wasn't tearing up the work of other grammarians, he made his own constructive suggestions for reform. One of my favourites of his ideas was to rename the exclamation point the 'eroteme', since it is a mark of passion. (From the Greek ἔρως [eros], meaning 'love' or 'desire'.)

not as a mere matter of personal taste or style, but now as a coherent system of knowledge. Accordingly, they termed grammar a 'science'. In the middle of the nineteenth century, however, a new wave of grammarians began to argue that grammar wasn't just a science in this broad sense of schematic knowledge, but a science in the narrower sense in which we use the word nowadays. To these new grammarians, their field was analogous to the natural sciences.

In staking this claim, the new grammarian-scientists were almost certainly reacting to protests from parents of schoolchildren and school officials, who claimed that the study of grammar was boring and ineffectual; pupils' time was better spent studying the natural sciences, which were exciting and taught *real* skills. Complaints about the mind-numbing uselessness of grammar surfaced as early as 1827, came to a boil by 1850, and persisted through the rest of the nineteenth century. If grammarians wanted to stay relevant and sell those lucrative grammar books to schools and their pupils, they needed to answer to carping parents and officials. In a few cases, grammarians peddled their wares with novelty methods and titles that smacked of circus-barker enthusiasm: British grammarian George Mudie perhaps epitomised this trend with his 1841 book, *The Grammar of the English Language truly* *made Easy by the Invention of Three Hundred Moveable Parts of Speech.* Truly, what could be easier or more fun than 300 moveable parts of speech?*

More often, however, grammarians answered to complaints about grammar's relative dullness and uselessness with rather ingenious rhetoric: grammar, they proposed, was a method of teaching students the art of scientific observation without requiring expensive or complex scientific apparatus. In service of this goal of teaching scientific skills, grammarians resolved to employ careful observation of English, because this gave them a way to use the methods of science to refine grammar; and they imported into their grammars some of the conventions of science textbooks, such as diagrams.

Rebel American grammarian Isaiah J. Morris emphasised the first approach – careful observation of English – in his 1858 *Morris's grammar: A philosophical and practical grammar of the English language, dialogically and*

---

* This title sounded so ridiculous to me that I was convinced it was a joke the first time I saw a reference to it in the long-defunct London newspaper *The Penny Satirist*. But it turns out that the book is very much real and Mudie was very much serious, and in typical nineteenth-century grammarian style, he talked plenty of trash about his peers' ostentation and the inefficiency of their methods.

PREFACE

It is often said that English Grammar is a lifetime study, and it is a fact not to be disguised, that students usually prosecute this branch of science for years, to little practical purpose, as grammar pupils rarely speak or write more correctly than others untaught. Now, grammar is unworthy of a lifetime study; life is too important, and labor and money are too precious to be thus invested, or, rather, wasted. "Time is money."—Dr. Franklin.

Is it not a little curious, that English Grammar should be a lifetime study? If so, who has yet mastered it? Who is competent to teach it? One would make rather an unprofitable effort, trying to teach what he did not understand himself. Would it not be more than unkind to require children to recite, and expect them to comprehend, what neither teachers nor authors understand, or can explain?

Isaiah J. Morris, 'offensive' from the very first page.

progressively arranged; in which every word is parsed according to its use.* Morris came out swinging from the start, distancing himself from reigning champions of grammar like the bestselling Samuel Kirkham. Kirkham and his ilk had relied on Greek and Latin grammar to come up with rules for English, and as a result, Morris fumed, they had littered the true 'laws of language' with 'errors' and

---

* Believe it or not, this is a relatively pithy title for a nineteenth-century book; some of them really took the term *title page* to be an imperative to fill the whole sheet.

'absurdities', which Morris was now left to 'expose and explode'. Correcting these mistakes was a moral obligation: 'Shall we roll sin under our tongues as a sweet morsel?' Morris demanded. 'It must be sin to teach what we know to be error.' In order to cleanse English grammars of these corruptions, Morris devoted the preface of his grammar to eviscerating the stale precepts of his predecessors. He knew that shredding such venerable grammarians would shock his readers: 'If the truth be disagreeable,' he shrugged, 'I choose to be offensive.'*

Morris offered a way to get beyond the deference to Latin and Greek that he believed had made earlier grammarians so error-prone: he advocated observing English carefully, and then making rules based on those observations, rather than trying to squeeze English grammar into frameworks designed for dead languages.† Grammar rules

---

* Morris is probably my favourite grammarian. What can I say? I like a sharp-spoken rebel.

† Morris, as a 'new grammarian' committed to observation of English, left Pope and Milton alone, unlike his predecessors. Instead of correcting the classics, the new generation of grammarians decided to amend each other's work instead, sometimes to absurd and comical effect. Alfred Ayres, a grammarian and elocutionist who edited an 1893 edition of *The English Grammar of William Cobbett*, praised the book as 'probably the most readable grammar ever written'.

would then arise directly from scrutinising English in action – and conveniently enough, the study of grammar would thus acquire for itself some of the virtues of the natural sciences that were being championed in the press, where commentators regularly argued that students were inherently inclined towards the observation and study of natural phenomena.

Grammarians had a second strategy to advance against critics who complained about the inferiority of grammar when compared to the natural sciences: the sentence diagram. Any good science textbook had diagrams, and if grammar was to be a science, it surely needed a system of schematic illustrations as well. And so in 1847, a grammarian named Stephen Clark introduced a system of diagrams designed to relate to the 'Science

---

Nonetheless, Ayres demurred, Cobbett's grammar had become a little bit dated in the fifty years that had passed since it was first printed. Ayres, as editor, felt it was his duty to repair Cobbett's mistakes by inserting bracketed corrections throughout the book. Thus Ayres turned this example sentence from Cobbett's original: 'And that it was this which made that false which would otherwise have been, and which was intended to be, true!' into: 'And that it was this which [that] made that false which [that] would otherwise have been, and which [that] was intended to be, true!' So much for Cobbett's vaunted 'readability'.

of Language' as maps did to geography, and figures to geometry and arithmetic. (It might sound odd to the modern reader to think of geography and geometry as natural sciences like physics and chemistry, but plenty of people back in Clark's days thought of them that way, and even people who didn't categorise those areas of study as 'sciences' believed the two disciplines were essential for the study of both the natural sciences and other respected fields like philosophy. And, unlike grammar, the mathematical sciences were considered 'perfect' and 'useful'.)

" The Lord uplifts his awful hand
And chains you to the shore."
(15.)

Compound sentence—transitive.

ANALYSIS.

Principal parts.
{ Lord—Subject of " uplifts " and " chains."
Uplifts }
[And] } Predicates of " Lord."
Chains }
Hand—Object of " uplifts."
You—Object of " chains." }

Adjuncts.
{ The—Adjunct of " Lord."
His }
Awful } Adjuncts of " hand."
To the shore—Adjunct of " chains." }

Clark's diagrams often made use of Bible verses: might as well pack in a few fearsome reminders about the powers of the Almighty for those schoolchildren misbehaving in the back of the class, after all.

The diagrams were a popular addition to grammar books, and held on for a long time. Although they've fallen out of pedagogical fashion these days, some readers may remember grammar classes from their childhoods that relied heavily on diagramming sentences on the blackboard. I certainly do, although I don't recall ever having to produce anything quite so comically elaborate as this humdinger.

EXAMPLES OF COMPLEX SENTENCES.

☞ **Rem.**—Let the pupil write the Diagram for each sentence on the black-board and insert the words in the proper places.

Blessed are the poor in spirit,
for theirs is the kingdom of heaven.
Blessed are they that mourn,
for they shall be comforted.
Blessed are the meek,
for they shall inherit the earth.
Blessed are they which do hunger and thirst
after righteousness, for they shall be filled.
Blessed are the pure in heart,
for they shall see God.
Blessed is the man that endureth temptation,
for, when he is tried,
he shall receive the crown of life,
which the Lord hath promised
to them that love him.

Clark, who invented the sentence-diagramming technique to visualise language, did his best to make the rest of his grammar follow the definitive-sounding, principle- and fact-heavy aesthetic of the natural sciences in other ways, too. Clark's rules were set up in an outline form, which Clark borrowed from his contemporary Peter Bullions. Bullions had used outlines to show his readers 'leading principles, definitions, and rules'. Those rules were to be displayed 'in larger type' to emphasise their importance; and exceptions to the rules were printed in type that got smaller and smaller the further away from an ironclad principle they crept.

In Bullions's nesting-doll fonts a fundamental tension is writ large: the conflicting demands of *rules* and *taste*. Bullions wrote that the purpose of punctuation was 'to convey to the reader an exact sense, and assist him in the proper delivery'. He warned, however, in a font two points smaller, that 'the duration of the pauses must be left to the taste of the reader or speaker'. Nevertheless, he then provided twenty-five rules and exceptions for the comma alone. These rules were then followed by yet another disclaimer in even tinier font than the first: 'The foregoing rules will, it is hoped, be found comprehensive; yet there may be some cases in which the student must rely on his own judgment.' Bullions seems to be equivocating, vacillating between committing to rules on the one hand, and capitulating to taste on the other.

Bullions's dilemma was *every* nineteenth-century grammarian's nightmare: how could it be possible to give

---

152   ENGLISH GRAMMAR.   § 88

466. The principal stops are the following:

The Comma (,) the semicolon (;) the colon (:) the period, or full stop (.) the note of interrogation (?) the note of exclamation (!)

467. The comma represents the shortest pause; the semicolon, a pause double that of the comma; the colon, double that of the semicolon; and the period, double that of the colon.

468. The duration of the pauses must be left to the taste of the

493. When, however, these phrases are not considered important, and particularly in short sentences, the comma is not inserted; as, " There is *surely* a pleasure in acting kindly." " Idleness *certainly* is the mother of all vices." " He was *at last* convinced of his error."

494. ₐ *ₐ The foregoing rules will, it is hoped, be found comprehensive; yet there may be some cases in which the student must rely on his own judgment.

Bullions and the tension between rules and taste.

useful rules for punctuation, while at the same time acknowledging that those rules couldn't describe every valid approach to punctuating a text? Whether a grammarian tried to police English with the laws of ancient Latin and Greek, or instead to derive his principles from examination of contemporary English in action, he could not escape the tension between the rigidity of rules and the flexibility of usage. Even if English writers' actual practices were taken into account and described in the rules, once laid down, the rules couldn't shift, while usage inevitably did. The grammarian was necessarily torn between trying (and inevitably failing) to anticipate every kind of usage, as Peter Bullions did with his twenty-five comma rules; or giving rules so general they were scarcely rules at all, the strategy Robert Lowth opted for with his specification that punctuation marks were successively longer pauses.* Mega-meta-grammarian Goold Brown, in

---

* People like Robert Lowth are typically termed 'prescriptivists', and grammarians like Isaiah Morris 'descriptivists'. Prescriptivists give rules about how language *ought* to be, while descriptivists want to observe and describe language. These categories are unfairly extreme in the case of nineteenth-century grammarians. They give the impression that supposed prescriptivists (like Lowth and his adherents) laid down laws without recognising that a writer's *taste* was still important, and they give the impression that supposed

his exhaustive *Grammar of English Grammars*, attempted to honey this problem with a bit of aspirational rhetoric:

> Some may begin to think that in treating of grammar we are dealing with something too various and changeable for the understanding to grasp; a dodging Proteus of the imagination, who is ever ready to assume some new shape, and elude the vigilance of the inquirer. But let the reader or student do his part; and, if he please, follow us with attention. We will endeavor, with welded links, to bind this Proteus, in such a manner that he shall neither escape from our hold, nor fail to give to the consulter an intelligible and satisfactory response. Be not discouraged, generous youth.

---

descriptivists (Morris and his ilk) just described language in action without trying to give any laws. The truth is much more complicated. All of these grammarians, negotiating the competing demands of rules and personal taste, were much more nuanced than dumping them into prescriptivist or descriptivist camps would indicate. In fact, one of the things that's most fascinating about reading grammars from Lowth's and Morris's times is how plain it is on the face of the texts that the grammarians were struggling with this fundamental problem of grammar.

Brown's labours may have been Herculean in scope, but they were still insufficient to solidify the fluid laws of grammar. Whenever grammarians tried to pin down punctuation marks with rules, they inevitably slipped their restraints, no matter whether they were shackled with a few broad rules or a hundred narrow ones. This Proteus didn't stop shifting shapes, it was just that now he had a heavy chain awkwardly dangling from his heels as he did so. The thorny relationship between rules and usage came to play a major role in the fate of our hero, the semicolon.

III

SEXY SEMICOLONS

In early spring of 1857, a writer for the *Chicago Daily Tribune* took a stroll through the streets of Chicago, making a note of facial hair trends for an article in the paper. Particularly popular was a moustache combined with a small goatee: 'Forty-three wore the moustache with a fancy tuft upon the chin, but with smooth cheeks; looking as if a semicolon was the best representation of their idea of facial adornment.'

The comparison was apt: semicolons were trendy in any form, follicular or literary.

For those of you accustomed to thinking about punctuation as subject to rules, it probably sounds odd to suggest that punctuation usage could be beholden to shifts in fashion. One of the virtues of rules would be to insulate us from whims and fancies. But even the originators of rule-based punctuation guides, the grammarians we encountered in the previous chapter, copped to punctuation's trendiness. As we've seen, they were conflicted about how best to negotiate the tension between rules and actual usage. As a result of their examination of usage, grammarians became keen observers of the punctuation whims of writers. The semicolon was on the rise in the 1800s, and its popularity might have been linked to the *un*fashionableness of two other marks, the parenthesis and the colon. By the early 1800s, parentheses were already *so* last century, inspiring T. O. Churchill's 1823 grammar to coolly pronounce that 'the parenthesis is now generally exploded as a deformity'. It got worse: three years later, the parenthesis had gone from Quasimodo to quasi ghost, with Rufus Nutting's *Practical Grammar* and Bradford Frazee's *Improved Grammar* both deeming it 'nearly obsolete'. The curved marks that humanist thinker Desiderius Erasmus had romantically called 'little moons' (lunulae) had crashed down to earth. By the mid-1800s, writers were also snubbing the colon: Oliver Felton's 1843 grammar fobbed it off with 'The COLON is now so seldom used by good writers, that rules for its use are unnecessary.' Seven years later, *The Common School Journal* gravely advised that when it came to colons, 'we should not let children use them', and 'should advise advanced scholars seldom to use them'.

This bad news for the colon was excellent news for the semicolon, however. It was the semicolon that writers substituted for its unstylish progenitor, and the semicolon soon surged through sentences at such a pace that it gobbled up not just most of the colons but a large share of commas as well. The semicolon had become so fashionable by the 1840s that Goold Brown leveraged its appeal to implore writers to reconsider the now-neglected colon. 'But who cannot perceive,' begged Brown, 'that without the colon, the semicolon becomes an absurdity? It can no longer be a semicolon, unless the half can remain when the whole is taken away!' Brown pointed out that there was really nothing wrong with the colon anyway; after all, he argued, colons, too, were 'once very fashionable'. (Brown himself was not, however, immune to the seductions of the semicolon: the first sentence of his massive grammar compendium contained seven of them, and nary a colon.)

Although Brown appealed to fashion in his plea for the colon, his argument offered a glimpse into the future of punctuation – the future we've inherited – in which logic reigns supreme in guides to punctuating. By the time renowned British grammarian H. W. Fowler published *A Dictionary of Modern English Usage*, in 1926, Brown's halves and wholes and absurdities had been pressed by Fowler into sterile language reminiscent of a *reductio* proof in mathematics, a curtly logical formulation in which neither fashion nor taste nor passion nor prosody had any part:

> The use of the semicolon to separate parallel expressions that would normally be separated by commas is not in itself illegitimate; but it must not be done when the expressions so separated form a group that is to be separated by nothing more than a comma, or not separated at all, from another part of the sentence; to do it is to make the less include the greater, which is absurd.

The semicolon had been transformed. Before the 1800s, it had been a pause. By the early 1800s, grammarians began to describe these pauses as means to delineate clauses properly, such that punctuation served syntax, with its prosodic and musical features secondary. By the mid-1800s, guided by a new generation of grammarians, grammar was tiptoeing towards a natural science model, deriving its rules from observation of English and teaching those rules to students through exercises in which they would be guided to make the same observations and draw general conclusions from them in the form of rules.

This process of moving from particular examples to general principles is known as 'induction'. Faced with the shift towards an inductive method modelled on science, mid-century grammarians waffled on the proper place of punctuation in their guidebooks. Was punctuation part of orthography, the study of how a language should be written? Was it part of prosody, how language should sound? Or did punctuation fall under the heading of syntax, the study of how language should be structured? The problem sparked vigorous debate. If punctuation were to be part of prosody, how could it be taught with the properly scientific inductive method? A student could hardly be expected to inductively derive rules from the rich, subtle, and infinitely varied rhythms that punctuation created in texts!

Uncertain of punctuation's proper classification, some grammarians simply left it out of their books entirely, sidestepping the problem of making rules that would be appropriate for an observation-based, natural science of language. Where punctuation *was* included in mid-1800s manuals, however, writers were given ample opportunity for semicolon use. In George Payn Quackenbos's 1862 *An English Grammar*, four possibilities for semicolon usage were given, and students were instructed to use a semicolon (not a colon, as we moderns would) to introduce a list of items.

---

264   THE SEMICOLON.

696. *Rule I.*—A semicolon must be placed between the members of compound sentences, unless the connection is exceedingly close; as "The wheel of fortune is ever turning; who can say, 'I shall be uppermost to-morrow'?"

If the members are very short, and the connection is close, the comma may be used in stead of the semicolon; as, "Man proposes, but God disposes."

697. *Rule II.*—A semicolon must be placed between the great divisions of sentences, when minor divisions occur that are separated by commas; as, "Plato called beauty a privilege of nature; Theocritus, a delightful prejudice."

698. *Rule III.*—A semicolon must be placed before an enumeration of particulars, when the names of the objects merely are given, without any formal introductory words; as, "There are three cases; the nominative, the possessive, and the objective."

699. *Rule IV.*—A semicolon must be placed before *&c.*, when it introduces an example; as at the close of the last paragraph.

Quackenbos's rules for the semicolon.

Nowadays all style guides advise against using a semi-colon to link together an independent and a dependent clause. In other words, the parts of a sentence separated by a semicolon must be able to stand on their own grammatically, so that they could be complete sentences if they wanted. But most nineteenth-century grammarians considered it perfectly acceptable to link together an independent and a dependent clause using a semicolon. If the author thought it sounded right, no need to meddle. As the grammarians' push towards logic, natural science, and induction continued, however, punctuation became decoupled from prosody and personal preference. By the 1880s, grammarians distinguished between rhetorical pauses, which were akin to pauses in speaking and were not to be marked by punctuation; and grammatical pauses, which required punctuation in order to make the structural and logical attributes of a sentence clear.

There were a few holdouts who resisted the new model of grammar. W. C. Fowler, for instance, advocated applying punctuation marks to signal rhetorical pauses, and in his 1881 grammar it was still permissible to use a semicolon between an independent and a dependent clause. But by his own admission, Fowler was the exception rather than the rule: by the time Fowler published his book, grammarians were treating the semicolon like a controlled substance. They generally prescribed them only for use between independent clauses, or to separate items in a list that were long enough to be subdivided with commas. An 1888 report on punctuation by the California State Board of Education called attention to the fact that there was 'but one use of the semicolon' in its lessons, its function restricted to separating independent clauses that contained commas. One hundred and thirty years had passed between Robert Lowth's grammar, which had envisioned punctuation marks as musical elements in prose, and this report, with its strict logic-based rules. In that time, the function of the semicolon had grown narrower and narrower until it had been whittled down to one or two applications.

This narrowing, as we've seen, happened in large part because grammar books were part of greater cultural and aesthetic trends in the Western world that privileged natural-scientific knowledge above other types of study; and in responding to those pressures, grammarians devised systems of punctuation that fitted comfortably with the ideals and the formats employed in science textbooks. Where had a century of rules, of grammars labelled 'true' and 'real' and 'improved', of grammars sidling up to natural science – where had all this got the generations of English speakers who had grown up immersed in books devoted to these principles? Into trouble, that's where, according to commentators. 'Where is the man that can tell why a comma is inserted instead of a semicolon; a semicolon, instead of a period [full stop]; a colon, instead of a period?' asked an 1899 American newspaper editorial. 'And yet, the science of punctuation is almost as definite as the science of mathematics, and, with few exceptions, a reason can be given for every mark inserted.' The rules were definitive, and yet their application varied wildly, and this divergence was apt to haunt a person all his or her life. As the *Boston Daily Globe* sombrely intoned:

> From childhood's earliest hour, or from that early hour in which one graduates from pothooks and hangers, and his wavering hand begins to form scraggly letters, those mysterious little hiero-glyphics that must be placed somewhere in every sentence confront him, and confuse him, and all through his natural life get him in trouble. Then, perhaps, after death his heirs will call each other names and invoke the courts of law because he were indiscreet enough to use a comma where he should have put a semicolon.

The *Globe* had good reason to raise the spectre of a punctuation-related legal battle; the new rule-based approach to punctuation had already begun to trouble the court system. Now it was not just the letter of the law but the punctuation separating those letters that judges and juries had to negotiate. Another commentator, for the *Indianapolis Journal*, concurred: citing four specific instances in which the semicolon had 'made trouble in the laws' by creating ambiguity in statutes, the author ascribed this trouble to 'inability to fix the function of the semicolon'. Old grammar books had given the rules of punctuation in terms of pauses, and 'if those who have been writing rules for punctuating compositions had stopped there, we would not have had all this trouble, but these teachers have been going on making new rules for years until no one can undertake to follow them, but each punctuates according to his pleasure, rather than his familiarity with the rules'. Finding the rules unhelpful, the public had run screaming in the opposite direction, punctuating willy-nilly. Therefore, the commentator opined, either the court system should write a legal treatise to define punctuation marks once and for all, or it should resolve to ignore punctuation altogether in its rulings.

But unbeknownst to the commentator, the American court system had already given the latter strategy a try, relying on old British case law for precedent. The Massachusetts Supreme Court had issued a ruling saying that punctuation had no part in statutes. This attempt to assert that Justice ought to extend her blindness to commas and semicolons was over-optimistic, and didn't obviate any of the interpretive problems with which the law had to contend. Any remaining hope that the law could somehow escape the challenges posed by punctuation went out the window when a semicolon set about wreaking havoc up and down the Northeast Corridor in a dramatic Massachusetts court case that caused six years of controversy in courtrooms, in legislative debates, and in the streets.

IV

LOOSE WOMEN AND LIQUOR LAWS

The Semicolon Wreaks Havoc in Boston

In late November 1900, a spat broke out in the city of Fall River, Massachusetts. 'It was an unimportant, picayune sort of a personal quarrel,' the *Chicago Tribune* reported, 'but it has had results of the greatest and most widespread importance.' The beginning of the story sounds like the start of a corny joke: a man walks into a bar at 11.10 p.m., sits down, and orders himself a drink. The bar owner, knowing that the man has been patronising a rival hotel bar, decides to spite him by refusing him his drink even though other patrons are still being served. Like any perfectly reasonable American denied a nightcap, the patron threatens to sue; and on the following day he

57

makes good on his threat by retaining the services of a lawyer. 'The lawyer brushed the dust off of [an] old statute, and there he found the semicolon – a dangerous, disastrous semicolon that would have been absolutely harmless, so far as the purposes of the wrangling Fall River citizen had been concerned, if only it had been a comma, which it wasn't.'

The statute the lawyer uncovered read: 'That no sale of spirituous or intoxicating liquor shall be made between the hours of 11 at night and 6 in the morning; nor during the Lord's day, except that if the licensee is also licensed as an Innholder he may supply such liquor to guests who have resorted to his house for food and lodging.' Pointing to the part of the statute preceding the semicolon, the lawyer filed an injunction against the Fall River hotel bar owner to prevent him from selling between 11 p.m. and 6 a.m. A local judge granted the injunction, whereupon the bar owner appealed the decision to the Massachusetts Supreme Court.

Standing in front of the justices of the Massachusetts Supreme Court, the bar owner's lawyer argued that the semicolon in the law 'was meant to be and should be construed, as a matter of fact, of being a comma'; and because the bar was situated inside a hotel, the innholder exception should therefore apply, because if the semicolon were construed as a comma, then the clause excepting innholders would negate *all* the rules stated in the statute. In support of his argument, the lawyer pointed out that when the law was originally passed, in 1875, it had contained a comma where the semicolon now intervened.

LAW AS ORIGINALLY PASSED (1875)	'SEMICOLONED' LAW (1880)
That no sale of spirituous or intoxicating liquor shall be made between the hours of 11 at night and 6 in the morning, nor during the Lord's day, except that if the licensee is also licensed as an Innholder he may supply such liquor to guests who have resorted to his house for food and lodging.	That no sale of spirituous or intoxicating liquor shall be made between the hours of 11 at night and 6 in the morning; nor during the Lord's day, except that if the licensee is also licensed as an Innholder he may supply such liquor to guests who have resorted to his house for food and lodging.

The original comma had been swapped to a semicolon when several years' worth of Massachusetts statutes were consolidated into one volume in 1880. Those consolidated statutes were presented to the Massachusetts legislature in 1881, and enacted with the semicolon in place. But the

1875 parchment original of the law, the barman's attorney insisted, clearly showed a comma, making the whole debacle an error of transcription.

Some further digging revealed, however, that the transcriptionist wasn't the culprit. The consolidated version of the laws had been written by Justice Charles H. Allen, who, the *Boston Daily Globe* observed, 'seemed to take a good bit of enjoyment out of the whole matter'. Allen had been transcribing from a *copy* of the original laws. Allen's copy of the laws was therefore twice removed from the original, and it turned out the semicolon had slipped in when some unknown person had created the intermediate copy from which Allen worked. But that wasn't to say that Justice Allen didn't tinker with the laws he was transcribing. The *Globe* pointed out that the transcribers openly acknowledged they had made some tweaks: 'It is expressly stated … in the preface to the commissioners' revision of the statutes that while they have in some instances changed the phraseology, there was no intention on the part of the commissioners to change the law, but that they intended to give it as they found it.'

Now it was up to the Massachusetts Supreme Court of 1900 to resolve the discrepancy between how the law had been 'found' and how it was presently 'given'. Their task was complicated by the fact that they had two opposite precedents they could use to justify their decision. On the one hand, there was precedent for calling the punctuation in a law determinative if it could 'throw light' on the meaning of the law. On the other hand, there was equal precedent for *ignoring* punctuation entirely: in an earlier ruling the court had decreed that 'punctuation may be disregarded'.

Years before this semicolon reared its head in Massachusetts, the US Supreme Court itself had weighed in on punctuation in a case that involved not going out for bourbon, but bringing home the bacon: when some pigs escaped from a farmer's pen one night and a neighbour found and boarded them for several days, the two men got into a dispute over whether the law required the owner of the pigs to reimburse their rescuer for room and board, and a comma in the relevant statutes played a key role in the case. 'The cause of all the trouble,' explained the *Boston Daily Globe*, 'was 10 hogs who strayed away from their comfortable, quiet sty one night, broke into the fields of literature, and became hopelessly entangled up with adverbs and commas.' The court reached a conclusion that was moderate in theory, but challengingly ambiguous in practice: 'Marks of punctuation may not control, but may aid in arriving at the meaning of the law.'

This slippery principle was captured as best it could be in the liquor law decision. The Massachusetts Supreme Court unanimously sided with the semicolon. The justices' first rationale for their decision was numerical: even though the original law had been passed with a comma, the revised and semicoloned law had been re-enacted repeatedly by the legislature. The semicolon had survived plenty of votes over the years, whereas the comma had only passed once. Further, the most recently published version of the statutes had given the law a title that seemed consonant with the meaning suggested by the semicolon: 'An Act to prohibit the sale of spirituous or intoxicating liquors between the hours of eleven at night and six in the morning.' Here the court once again veered away from the original version of the law, which had no such title.

Police were ordered to start enforcing the newly unearthed law immediately. Chaos descended on Boston. The public was outraged, hotel owners were outraged, and liquor distributors were outraged. Almost immediately, everyone who had an interest in the sale of booze began organising in order to appeal to the state legislature to amend the statute on the very first day it was back in session. Accordingly, a bill to amend what had become popularly known as the 'Semicolon Law' came before the Massachusetts Senate in April 1901. Senator Fitzgerald of

Suffolk County argued in favour of the amendment, contending that 'the proposition before the senate was to place the law as nearly as possible where it was when it was first enacted'. But fellow Suffolk senator Mr Howland argued that the Supreme Court had been correct in looking to the title of the statute to discern the legislature's intent, and he opposed the amendment. Senator Huntress of Middlesex County, on the other hand, didn't give a damn what the intention of the legislature had been: the question was whether the proposed amendment was 'better for the general welfare of the whole community' than the Semicolon Law, and he reckoned it wasn't. A vote was taken, and the amendment failed 21 to 10. The semicolon stood.

The predicament in Massachusetts began to attract national attention. A commentator for the *Washington Post*, covering the situation on the ground in Boston, wryly noted that the Semicolon Law was now 'well known throughout the country, owing to the great wailing and gnashing of teeth from this Commonwealth'. Bostonians weren't about to kowtow to 'misfit commas and semicolons', and enterprising drinkers quickly found ways to exploit loopholes in the enforcement of the Semicolon Law. If liquor wasn't going to be sold after eleven o'clock, then why not just buy as much liquor as possible before the cut-off? There was no rule that said you couldn't go on *drinking* the booze after eleven. This attitude turned buying alcohol into a kind of competitive sport: Bostonians raced to get to restaurants as early as possible, staked out tables, and then tried to 'order up the whole wine list' so that they would be adequately provisioned for the entire night. The poor souls who dared to go to the theatre before dinner thus found it nearly impossible to find a seat in a restaurant after the show finished – and even if a seat *could* be found, the latecomers would have to settle for alcohol-free 'temperance drinks', since by that point all the booze was sold out and making its way down the eager throats of the people who got to the restaurant right at opening time.

'It is a peculiar failing of man,' the *Post*'s correspondent sagely observed, '… that whatever is denied him, that he most earnestly desires.' The threat of being unable to order alcohol after 11 p.m. meant that 'men who at home in other cities where liquor flows like water are temperate and even abstemious – when they land in Boston after 11 o'clock are transformed into seeming dipsomaniacs. In other words, the minute they find out they cannot get a drink, they are willing to commit anything short of manslaughter to get one.' Every Saturday night, the whole of New England 'bore a distinct resemblance to the Fourth of July', the commentator added. Commuter trains serving the region were standing-room only, stuffed to the gills with drunks of all descriptions. 'The life of the latter-day Puritan,' the *Post* concluded, 'is not entirely devoid of alcoholic glee.'

But this ethanol-fuelled, Independence Day-style revelry was not bacchanalian enough for opponents of the Semicolon Law, who continued to lobby fiercely for an amendment to the statute. Advocates of the law, on the other hand, pointed to the raucous behaviour of Massachusetts drunks as proof positive that alcohol was a bad influence. If this was how Bostonians behaved when they had *fewer* hours of liquor-buying time, who knew to what depths they might sink if given unfettered access to alcohol? The battle between the pro- and anti-Semicolon Law camps roared vigorously on. This was great news for another punctuation mark, the exclamation mark, since the Semicolon Law was 'the greatest provoker of profanity yet invented'.

Profane exclamations from Massachusetts citizens spurred the legislature to form a liquor law committee tasked with scrutinising the Semicolon Law. In 1904, the committee proposed a revised law that would allow innkeepers to sell alcohol until midnight, but would prevent them from going back to selling all night long, as they had done before the Semicolon Law was unearthed in the first place. This revision would mean that the statute would return to its original 1875 form, with a comma instead of a semicolon. Arguments both for and against were impassioned. 'If every member of this house would vote as he drank,' sniped Representative Davis of Salem, '[the bill to repeal the Semicolon Law] would be adopted by a large majority.' Nevertheless, it failed, 57 to 132.

The matter was far from closed, however. In February 1905, the Liquor Law Committee convened a group of 'friends and foes of the semicolon' to discuss the law. For neither the first nor the last time in history, a bunch of men sat around in a room fretting that, given a taste of any kind of freedom (in this case, in the form of liquor), women might ride off the rails of decency. Arguments went on all day long, and tended towards hyperbole. If 'liquor dealers' were allowed one extra hour to sell booze, a Baptist minister testified, it would 'cause the downfall of dozens, scores, yes, even hundreds of young women in an increased degree'. The pastor came by this opinion from having visited second-class hotels and 'dance' halls – but these visits to questionable establishments, he hastened to add, were made purely from 'a humanitarian standpoint'. After the minister spoke, a representative for the Massachusetts Hotel Association, the Wine and Spirit Dealers' Association, and the Brewers' Association pleaded the opposite position. 'All we ask is that innholders may sell liquor to their guests one hour longer at night,' the representative explained. 'We don't want the semicolon law abolished, and I hope the word "semicolon" won't be mentioned during the hearing. We're not petitioning for any change in punctuation. We simply want one hour more.' One temperance advocate, B. B. Johnson, advocated instead for one hour *less*: citing a Glaswegian law that had dialled back liquor hours and thereby cut down on drunkenness, he suggested liquor sales should end at 10 p.m., not 11 p.m., as the Semicolon Law specified. 'Are you in favor of the sale of liquor at all?' one of the Hotel Association attorneys demanded, outraged by this new proposal to restrict the sale hours even more. 'Only when it is needed as an antidote for disease,' Johnson piously responded.

Finally, after years of fighting, the legislature passed the proposed amendment, which was then put to a popular vote on 11 December 1906. The people of Massachusetts approved. This delighted the mayor of Boston, John F. Fitzgerald,* who saw the amended statute

---

* Mayor Fitzgerald, known as 'Honey Fitz' for his smooth talking and his sweet singing voice, was future US President John F. Kennedy's maternal grandfather. JFK's paternal line had an interest in liquor as well: Joseph Kennedy, JFK's father, made his fortune from distributing Scotch whisky. 'Honey

as a victory for 'good sense and progressiveness' over 'provincialism'. Good sense or not, it was not clear that the new regulations made any real difference in the drinking habits of Massachusetts residents; the *New York Sun* snickered that on the night the act went into effect, scarcely anyone was seen availing him- or herself of the extra hour of drinking time:

> At last the 'lid' was lifted. Boston was to be 'gay'. New York and the devil were no longer to have all the fun ... Dionysus, ever young and fair, was to come out of the Art museum and ride tigerback through the restaurants ... The home of thought was to be the palace of sport ... [But] Bostonians are happier under restraint.

Apparently the wry commentator in the *Washington Post* had been right: people liked their liquor to play hard to

---

Fitz' Fitzgerald has a cocktail named after him – a version of the daiquiri, in a nod to his famous grandson's favourite tipple. If you want to try one out, shake up 1½ fl. oz aged rum, ¾ fl. oz honey syrup, ¾ fl. oz fresh grapefruit juice, and 2 dashes of Peychaud's bitters with ice. Better make it a double if you're going directly on to the next chapter, where punctuation in the law takes a macabre turn.

get. Still, even if alcohol consumption hadn't perceptibly increased after the law was amended, Massachusetts hotel owners felt they had cause to celebrate at their November 1909 banquet: former Senator W. A. Morse of Cape Cod said that when he had last attended the banquet, 'members of the association were suffering from some errors of grammar in the laws of the state, but now they were not worried by either commas or semicolons'.

Maybe the Boston liquor men were no longer worried about punctuation, but the legal system certainly still was – and is.

POWER OF POINTS

Punctuation That Upset Work of Solons.

Comma or Semicolon Has Spoiled the Statutes.

Legal Decisions That Have Settled Colons.

Massachusetts and Ohio Cases Noted.

Baltimore Man Failed to Pay a Bill with a Semicolon.

V

THE MINUTIAE
OF MERCY

The troubling questions of interpretation and intent that
the Semicolon Law dredged up still haunt the law. Twenty-
first-century legal thinking on the question of punctuation is ostensibly just an amplified version of the competing principles the Massachusetts Supreme Court weighed
as it wrestled with the Semicolon Law case. 'The modern
Court recognizes that grammar and punctuation often
clarify meaning,' allows a 2010 guide to statutory interpretation in the United States. Yet in determining a statute's 'true meaning', 'the Court remains reluctant ... to
place primary importance on punctuation' – and no
wonder, when there is ample precedent for invoking

centuries-old British law that asserted that 'punctuation is no part of a statute'. Relying on this venerable principle of legal hermeneutics, the US Supreme Court has ruled, for instance, that 'punctuation is the most fallible standard by which to interpret a writing'. Taking it even further, courts have opined that 'punctuation is no part of the English language'.

That latter proclamation that punctuation marks are not even part of the language you are reading right this very second seems utterly ridiculous at first but with some effort you can imagine where the idea comes from its perfectly possible to read writing with no punctuation whatsoever and understand it sure it slows you down and is pretty annoying but you damn well know what Im saying here dont you the fact is that its only in some cases that punctuation is or even could be dispositive.*

---

* Mark Twain, famously defensive of his right to punctuate exactly how he wanted to, purportedly grew weary of criticism of his sometimes unconventional choices and published a piece of writing that was wholly without punctuation marks, but with a string of commas, semicolons, and other marks at the bottom of the text, along with a note telling the reader to put them where he or she pleased since Twain clearly couldn't be trusted with them. (The sources that mention this piece report it variously as a letter or as a short story; I have yet to find the Twain composition that matches this description.)

Certainly when considering oral testimony that has been transcribed by a court reporter, there might be grounds to disregard punctuation in attempting to figure out what was said. But even so, the guidelines I just quoted don't make much sense. For one thing, *some* punctuation marks can be considered shorthand for words. If I tell you that I want you to pick up some flour, eggs and milk, the comma after flour pretty much means 'and'. It's really not clear that that comma is any different in status than a word. So everything ends up hanging on some person or persons determining what the 'true meaning' of a statement is, and what kind of nebulous standard is *that* for a discipline of precision, which the law fancies itself to be?

Since it's not always easy to toss out punctuation as not 'part of the English language', it's really no wonder that entire cases regularly revolve around one tiny punctuation mark. In Ohio, a woman gets out of a parking ticket because of a forgotten comma. In the Philippines, the result of a mayoral election is voided because the court chooses to disregard a 'semi-colon which the appellant views with a respect bordering on fetishism'.* Cases like these are two a penny. But the stakes have sometimes been

---

* So much for trying to get off on a technicality!

much higher than traffic tickets or cocktails after 11 p.m. or even election results. Men have lost their lives as a result of punctuation.

In the early hours of 3 August 1916, Sir Roger Casement, formerly a diplomat for the English Crown, was hanged for treason. He had been arrested just four months earlier, and charged with helping to mastermind the Irish republicans' Easter Rising. Casement himself never made it to his rendezvous with the other leaders of the rebellion; he was arrested shortly after making landfall in Ballyheigue Bay in a dinghy that had pushed off from a German U-boat. Indeed, Casement's plotting had occurred on German soil and with German backing: in 1914, three years after he had retired from the diplomatic service and been knighted, he was said to have turned up at the Limburg Lahn prison camp to attempt to persuade Irish prisoners of war to fight against British rule with support from Germany.

At trial, the fact that Casement's conniving occurred in Germany was crucial to the defence's case. Since the indictment made it clear that Casement's activities in Germany were those for which he was accused of treason – after all, he had only just landed his boat on British soil, in County Kerry, when he was arrested – Casement's lawyer, Sergeant A. M. Sullivan, argued that the treason law did not apply. The Treason Act of 1351 on which Casement's charges were based read in part:

> if a Man do levy War against our Lord the King
> in his Realm, or be adherent to the King's Enemies
> in his Realm, giving to them Aid and Comfort in
> the Realm, or elsewhere, and thereof be probably
> attainted of open Deed by the People of their
> Condition: …, and if a Man slea the Chancellor,
> Treasurer, or the King's Justices of the one Bench
> or the other, Justices in Eyre, or Justices of Assise,
> and all other Justices assigned to hear and deter-
> mine, being in their Places, doing their Offices:
> And it is to be understood, that in the Cases above
> rehearsed, that ought to be judged Treason which
> extends to our Lord the King, and his Royal
> Majesty: …

Prosecutors argued that Casement had clearly been giving 'aid and comfort' to the Crown's enemies while they were in Germany, and was therefore guilty under the Treason Act for assisting the Crown's enemies 'elsewhere'. But Sullivan argued that his client was not guilty under the Act: in his reading of the law, the accused had to be 'adher-ent' to the Crown's enemy while the accused himself was 'in his Realm', i.e., in Britain. In other words, because the indictment only accused Casement of aiding the enemy while he was on *German* soil, his acts didn't fall under the purview of the Treason Act.

The Crown's prosecutor countered that the comma before 'or elsewhere' was fatal to the defence's argument; couldn't 'or elsewhere' simply refer back to the clauses about adhering to the Crown's enemies, after all? Sullivan was quick to pounce on this proposition, pointing out that the original statutes were unpunctuated, and reminding the court that precedent dictated that punctuation be ignored anyway in interpreting a statute. Sans punctuation, Sullivan's construction of the statute was perfectly reasonable. But the judge sided with the prosecution anyway, and Sullivan was left to make his argument again on appeal.

Before the appeals court, Sullivan's argument seemed to be going well until he was suddenly interrupted by Justice Darling, who announced that he and his brother had gone to have a look at the original Norman-French statute roll in which the Treason Act was contained, and that he had 'carefully observed the writing and the punctuation'. This was more than a little surprising, since fourteenth-century statutes had always been thought not to have any punctuation. The Justice went on, clarifying that the 'punctuation' to which he referred was a transverse line* positioned in the same place as the contentious comma in the parliamentary rolls.† This, the Justice concluded, must signal that the original statute had the sense that the Crown prosecutor had imputed to it.

This argument was questionable on many levels, but Sullivan chose to attack it on probably the most sensible grounds: whether the original statute was punctuated or not could have no bearing on the matter at hand, because the court had repeatedly opined that punctuation was not to be regarded as dispositive. It was a solid argument, but the justices upheld the initial guilty verdict regardless. So it has come to be said that Sir Roger Casement was 'hanged on a comma'.‡

---

* It sounds like Darling was describing a *virgula suspensiva*, sometimes used in place of a comma but also as a more general 'pause' mark at the time the Treason Act was penned.

† There was another break in the French statute, the Justice noted, but after examination with a magnifying glass he and his brother concluded it was an artefact of the folding of the paper over many centuries.

‡ Like most good catchprases, this is hyperbole. The decision the court issued laid primary emphasis on the fact that the courts had enforced the comma'd reading of the treason law in many previous cases. Still, it's undoubtedly true that the question of the comma mattered: if it hadn't, Justice Darling

It has not always been the presence of a punctuation mark but sometimes its yawning *absence* that has troubled the Western legal system. A particularly heart-wrenching case that was tried on the cusp of the Great Depression in America painfully illustrates the problems that can be caused by a missing semicolon. In 1927, two men were convicted of murder in New Jersey. The jury's verdict and sentencing recommendation was written as follows: 'We find the defendant, Salvatore Merra, guilty of murder in the first degree, and the defendant, Salvatore Rannelli,

---

wouldn't have spent time examining the 1351 original of the Act with a magnifying glass. Further, as Sullivan pointed out, there was also precedent for ignoring punctuation; thus it seems a choice was made to privilege one stack of precedents over another.

During the trial and appeal, Casement's plight attracted support in both the UK and the US. Many people felt his sentence was unjust and ought to be commuted. In response, the British government leaked passages alleged to be from Casement's diaries of his homosexual encounters, on the assumption that no one would defend a gay man. Sadly they were correct: support for Casement thinned. The authenticity of the diaries, known as the 'Black Diaries', is a matter of some controversy, but what will be important to this chapter's consideration of cases like Casement's is the fact that they were used successfully to put off his supporters. See Kevin Grant, 'Roger Casement: gay Irish martyr or a victim of a British forgery?', *Guardian* (28 September 2016).

guilty of murder in the first degree and recommend life imprisonment at hard labor.' The judge interpreted the life imprisonment recommendation as applicable only to Rannelli, since that recommendation followed only the repetition of 'guilty of murder in the first degree' after Rannelli's name. Using this reasoning, the judge sentenced Salvatore Merra to death for the same crime. In an eleventh-hour appeal, Merra's lawyer (and New Jersey senator) Alexander Simpson argued that the jury meant the life imprisonment recommendation to apply to both men – otherwise, the jurors would surely have used a semicolon to separate their verdict on Merra from their verdict on Rannelli, so that the verdict would have read: 'We find the defendant, Salvatore Merra, guilty of murder in the first degree; and the defendant, Salvatore Rannelli, guilty of murder in the first degree and recommend life imprisonment at hard labor.' The prosecution, on the other hand, countered that the jury clearly intended for Merra to die.

When the case was heard by the Court of Errors and Appeals of New Jersey, all but two members of the court voted to uphold the death sentence. Their votes reveal a jaw-droppingly wilful blindness to facts that ought to have spared Merra. In his dissenting opinion, Justice Samuel Kalisch noted that the verdict as originally recorded at trial read: 'We find the defendant Salvatore Merra guilty of murder in the first degree and the defendant Salvatore Rannelli guilty of murder in the first degree, and recommend life imprisonment at hard labor.' Further, the jury was polled after the verdict and each juror repeated: 'I find the defendant Salvatore Merra guilty of murder in the first degree and the defendant Salvatore Rannelli guilty of murder in the first degree and recommend life imprisonment.' And the trial judge, on petition, had certified the verdict as recorded. And yet now, many months after the trial took place, the presiding judge (who had become aware of Senator Simpson's semicolon argument) suddenly insisted that the recorded verdict he had certified was 'not an accurate statement of the verdict rendered by the jury', and he 'rectified' the verdict by adding new punctuation and swapping a 'we find' for an 'and': 'We find the defendant Salvatore Merra guilty of murder in the first degree. We find the defendant Salvatore Rannelli guilty of murder in the first degree, and recommend life imprisonment at hard labor.' And there was even more reason than judicial shenanigans to err on the side of life imprisonment: New Jersey juries were required to make an explicit recommendation of either death or life imprisonment in first-degree murder convictions. The fact that the verdict makes explicit mention only of life imprisonment should have meant that life imprisonment was the sentence recommended for *both* men.

Kalisch's disdain for the trial judge in his dissenting opinion is clear, and the chilling conclusion he draws is worth dwelling on:

> It does not appear that the trial judge had any notes of what the verdict was and the only inference is that he must have resorted to occult means, in order to recall the intonation of the voice of the foreman of the jury, his hesitation and pauses in order to portray what took place. To countenance such interference with verdicts of a jury, especially in a case involving life, is a serious inroad on the right of trial by jury. It renders verdicts unstable and leaves a citizen accused of crime at the mercy of judicial oppression … I am unwilling to consign a human being to death on any such hair splitting refinement.

Merra's appeal travelled upwards through the hierarchy of courts, finally making its way to the summer residence of United States Supreme Court Justice Louis Brandeis. Brandeis, perched in his classic Cape house overlooking Oyster Bay River in Massachusetts, reviewed the documents but declined to grant a writ of error. Merra went to the electric chair three days after marrying the mother of his two-and-a-half-year-old son a few feet away from the death chamber. Speaking in Italian to an 'unusually large' crowd gathered to watch him die – the jailhouse wedding had amplified interest in his case – he protested his innocence until the last, but to no avail. The justices up and down the court system who authorised Merra's execution had determined that the true meaning of the original verdict indicated Merra must die. What are we to make of the disturbing fact that dissenting justices found an *opposite* intelligible meaning?*

---

* The Merra decision, it is worth noting, is cited in numerous United States court cases post-Merra. The law in both America and the United Kingdom relies on precedent; its past is very often our present. Equally, and perhaps much more alarmingly in America, which is one of only two first-world nations along with Japan still to retain capital punishment, the Merra case is not the only punctuation-related death-penalty case in which an appeals court has lavished special powers and privileges on the trial judge. In *People v Huggins*, a 2006 appeal case, the court examined evidence that the judge may have misinstructed the jury as to the criteria for competence to stand trial. The court transcript showed punctuation that differed from the standard instructions, but more seriously, it showed omission of a significant conjunction, an '*and*' that was critical to the meaning of the instructions. The majority

Aha! you might be thinking. *So it's true what all the memes say: punctuation* is *a matter of life and death. 'Let's eat grandma' really might result in somebody chowing down on a nice old lady, instead of summoning her to the dinner table as 'Let's eat, grandma' would. Let's keep our commas and semi-colons where the rules say they should be, and everything will be fine.* Unfortunately it isn't that simple, and the message of these cases is much darker. The moral of Merra's story is that no matter how precise you are with your punctuation, and no matter how carefully constructed the legal rules for punctuation use and interpretation might be, there will almost always be a way to cast doubt on the origins of a punctuation mark, or on its original intended meaning, or on its most valid construction given its context. A zealous attorney might well be able to find a way to make

---

opinion concludes that 'it is inconceivable that the trial court misread the instruction in the nonsensical manner reflected by the punctuation supplied by the court reporter'. Lone dissenter Justice Kennard pointed out how fallacious it is to assume a judge is incapable of error in such a matter, but he did so without pointing out the broader implications of this kind of decision. We should pay attention to those broader implications: what does it mean for jury systems and democracies that a trial judge is deferred to over a jury, or over the available evidence? See *People v Huggins*, 175 38 Cal.4th 175; 41 Cal.Rptr.3d 593; 131 P.3d 995 [April 2006].

'Let's eat, grandma' justify sticking a fork in her, particularly if the judge and jury already have cannibalistic tendencies.

Bias matters, and it matters more than most of us would like to believe it does when it comes to institutions we're supposed to trust, like our legal systems. Salvatore Merra, for instance, and his convicted co-defendant, Salvatore Rannelli, had found themselves on trial at perhaps the worst possible time. Their original trial took place in 1926, and their appeal in the spring and early summer of 1927. The two men, Italian immigrants, were accused of murdering a paymaster in the course of a robbery. Their convictions for that crime took place in the shadow of one of the twentieth century's most notorious cases: the trial and conviction of Nicola Sacco and Bartolomeo Vanzetti. Sacco and Vanzetti were also Italian immigrants. They were also accused of murdering a paymaster in the course of a robbery.* The jury had convicted Sacco and Vanzetti after just a few hours' deliberation, but irregularities in the trial prompted appeals

---

* Sacco and Vanzetti were anarchists as well, which didn't help them one bit. The presiding judge referred to them as 'anarchistic bastards'. See Eric Foner, 'Sacco and Vanzetti', *The Nation*, 20 August 1977, p. 137.

and protests from people around the globe urging that the verdict be overturned. Sacco and Vanzetti's supporters were fighting against intense anti-Italian and anti-immigrant sentiment. The governor of Massachusetts formed a committee to consider executive clemency for the two convicted men. The clemency committee was headed by the then-president of Harvard University, Abbott Lawrence Lowell, whose career highlights included a stint as an official of the Immigration Restriction League, and the enforcement of segregation on the Harvard campus. When the Lowell Committee, which deliberated behind closed doors, emerged to declare that the trial had been fair after all, journalist Heywood Broun remarked with wry wrath: 'What more can two immigrants from Italy expect? It is not every prisoner who has a president of Harvard throw on the switch for him.'

Was Salvatore Merra's fate in part a product of those same prejudices of the time? Was Sir Roger Casement's conviction for treason a fait accompli because of his Irish nationalism and his alleged homosexuality? It's tempting to ask, too, if the enforcement of the Semicolon Law in the United States had something to do with anti-Irish sentiment in Massachusetts, where the Irish were stereotyped as (among other things) drunks. (Think of the

American colloquialism for a police van: *paddy wagon*.) The owner of the bar in Fall River who was sued for selling drink after 11 p.m. had the surname Kelley. Of course, that doesn't necessarily mean he was of Irish extraction, and even if he was, it doesn't necessarily mean that the decision of the court was motivated by bigotry. It could be coincidence. But such coincidences deserve our attention and our vigilance. So many discrete racist or otherwise malignantly biased acts can be excused as meaningless matters of happenstance, just as a puzzle piece looks like an abstract blob of nothing until hundreds of them are assembled all together and then suddenly – we see.

In one of Shakespeare's most famous scenes, which forms the climax of *The Merchant of Venice*, the beautiful Portia cross-dresses* to appear in court posing as a lawyer in an attempt to save her husband's friend, Antonio. Portia's husband, Bassanio, has defaulted on a loan from Jewish merchant Shylock, and as guarantor for the loan, Antonio must pay the price: per their contract, Shylock may take from him a pound of flesh. Appealing to Shylock, Portia makes a lofty plea. 'The quality of mercy is not

---

* In the 2004 film of the play, she is wearing the type of facial hair that the newspaper reporter at the beginning of Chapter Three described as a semicolon.

strained,' she begins. 'It droppeth as the gentle rain from heaven upon the place beneath.' She goes on in this vein, singing the praises of mercy, and finally asking Shylock to be merciful. 'I want the law,' Shylock replies, resolute. And so Portia gives him the law: the terms of the contract specify that if Bassanio were to default, Shylock may collect a pound of flesh from Antonio. But, Portia cautions, the amount specified is exact. Shylock may take no more and no less than a pound, and he may take only flesh, not blood: is he certain he can be so accurate? Portia reminds him of the consequences should he err. 'If the scale do turn, But in the estimation of a hair, Thou diest and all thy goods are confiscate.' Shylock, defeated, relents. In *The Merchant of Venice*, it isn't a pie-in-the-sky ideal of mercy that tips figurative scales of justice, but the threat of real flesh tipping real metal scales that determines the outcome of the trial. If there is mercy in the outcome for Antonio, it is an incidental by-product of precision.

The Merchant of Venice, although fiction, illustrates a fundamental truth of the law: it turns on technicality and precision. To some degree, it *must*: if the law is intended to be accessible to the people to whom it accords freedoms and restrictions, those people ought to be able to understand it clearly. But no matter how technically precise and careful, the law will always be subject to interpretation. It is often the case that more than one interpretation of the letter of the law is available to us, so that justices disposed to keep bars open or close them down could both find a rationale for doing so. Just so with the justices disposed to save or execute Salvatore Merra. And does anyone imagine, in an alternative *Merchant of Venice* in which the debtor was the Jew and the lender a Christian, that the pound of flesh wouldn't have been paid in Shakespeare's era? Perhaps in such an alternative version of the play, there would be mutterings from the bench about the 'spirit' or 'original intent' of the contract Bassanio, Antonio, and Shylock entered into. To imagine that the law is safe from the biases of one's time – be they the prejudices of sixteenth-century Venice, or twentieth-century New Jersey, or in our courtrooms today – is a dangerous dream.

The law is skeletal, a mere naked framework of words, and those words require interpretation for the law to become animate and to act in the world. Any time interpretation is involved (which really means: any time a human being gets involved in *anything*), there is the opportunity for our best and most beautiful qualities to inflect the material we are interpreting – but there is equally the opportunity for our cynicism, our racism, and our little hatreds and bigotries to be exercised through the application of laws that are, at the end of the day, inert tools that must be wielded by someone to construct a more or less merciful world. Any other vision of our laws – any vision in which they are perfect and complete and speak for themselves – is fantasy. In most cases, perhaps all cases, there will be an opportunity to act ungenerously, and to let some Salvatore Merra go to the chair, or instead to take the opportunity to choose a more merciful path. Given this reality, there is no easy answer to questions of interpretation in the law, and statutory guidebooks that tell us the 'rules of legal hermeneutics' will find that those interpretive rules, much like the rules of grammar books, quickly meet challenges from the complex irreducibilities of the real world. Perhaps the only thing that can be advised is that anyone charged with application of the law – a judge, a juror, a lawyer – should be always encouraging the better angels of our nature, and constantly on the lookout for the worse devils in it.

CARVING SEMICOLONS IN STONE

What was to be the fate of the semicolon, breaker of Bostonian spirits, and the rules that aimed to bring it to heel? In the same year the Massachusetts Semicolon Law was repealed, 1906, the Chicago Press published a two-hundred-page style guide called *Manual of Style*. Unlike the grammar textbooks of the nineteenth century, this book was not for schoolchildren, but for authors, editors, and proofreaders. Shift in audience notwithstanding, the *Manual* inherited both the nineteenth century's predilection for rules, and its worries about trends. As the *Manual* put it, 'Rules and regulations such as these, in the nature of the case, cannot be endowed with the fixity of rock-ribbed law. They are meant for the average case, and must be applied with a certain degree of elasticity.' The *Manual* presented its rules in numbered form, with nineteen regulations given for the most commonly used punctuation mark, the comma.

The disclaimer about 'elasticity' was still being repeated over a century later in the sixteenth iteration of the *Manual*. It had 'become a maxim', and was enshrined in the preface of every edition of the *Manual*.* But the rest of the book had changed considerably since it was first printed, with its major revisions pushing it further and further along the course first plotted by those nineteenth-century rule setters. In the thirteenth edition, published in 1982, *A Manual of Style* became *The Chicago Manual of Style*, which was 'what everybody else calls it', and an apt reflection of the authority the book had achieved by dominating the market for style books. With the definite article

---

* There is now a seventeenth edition of the *Manual* (1,144 pages, 40 comma rules), but its preface is almost exclusively taken up with reflections on changes necessitated by new writing and reading technologies, such as digital publishing and social media. At the end of the preface, however, the editors take care to mention that the seventeenth edition is still guided 'by the principles that have been handed down through earlier editions'. Presumably 'elasticity' remains among them.

came a shift towards greater definitiveness all around: this was 'much more a "how-to" book for authors and editors than was its predecessor'. Still, the *Manual* at least paid some lip service to taste: 'Punctuation should be governed by its function, which is to make the author's meaning clear, to promote ease of reading, and in varying degrees to contribute to the author's style.' There was no indication of *how* punctuation might contribute to style, and writers were warned that rules should be followed to regulate the presence of 'the subjective element'.

The sixteenth edition of the *Manual* (1,026 pages, 37 comma rules) carried these principles still further away from that 'subjective element': the preface announced that the book would 'recommend a single rule for a given stylistic matter rather than presenting multiple options'. Exceptions were eliminated where possible. This was what the *Manual*'s users wanted, though it's unclear whether firmer and more numerous rules really reduced uncertainty, if *The Chicago Manual of Style*'s popular 'Chicago Style Q&A' web page is any indication. On the site, anyone can write in with questions about how the rules are to be applied, and learn that if the *Manual* hasn't got the exact construction they are looking for, they can 'extrapolate' from the rules that are given. Meanwhile, in the pages of the current edition of the *Manual*, authorial 'style' has disappeared entirely from the punctuation section; instead, the punctuation rules the *Manual* gives are celebrated as the 'logical application of traditional practice'. Has *The Manual of Style* lost its sense of style?

Whether it's the *Manual* that peers down from your bookshelf, or Strunk and White, or the APA (American Psychological Association) style guide, or Fowler, or Lynne Truss, it's fair to ask why we consider these books authoritative, and if there might not be some better way to assess our writing than through their dicta. It seems that style books in any language aren't successfully clearing up ambiguities: Harun Küçük, a professor at the University of Pennsylvania, tells me that the semicolon is used in Turkish and Arabic too, and that writers in those languages aren't any less confused about its usage than writers in English are. Other people grope for something better than what's offered in style guides; over dinner in Berlin, my friends James Harker and Paul Festa decide that the semicolon is 'the California stop* of punctu-

---

* Californians are notorious amongst Americans for applying their generally laid-back attitudes to the observance of traffic laws; hence a 'California stop' refers to the practice of slowing at the sight of a stop sign but never fully coming to a halt, with the driver hitting the gas as soon as they determine they can dart through the intersection unscathed.

ation'. Still others obviate the question of semicolon usage entirely: Tim Casey, an abstract painter and writer who grew up in the American Southwest, tells me that 'in Texas they (we) use the term "Golly" as a universal form of punctuated pause within the clause'. I don't know if I could get along solely on *Golly*s, but as I stare down bookshelves bowed under the weight of umpteen conflicting and competing style guides, golly is it tempting to give it a try.

SEMICOLON SAVANTS

Humourist Mark Twain wasn't averse to a 'golly' or two in some of the dialogue in his books, but for anyone who dared to interfere with his punctuation, he had stronger words. 'The damned half-developed foetus!' Twain raged to his UK publishers Chatto & Windus. Once again, Twain was excoriating a proofreader, a professional figure who frequently met with his wrath. Ninety per cent of the 'labor & vexation' of writing, Twain insisted, 'consists in annihilating their ignorant & purposeless punctuation & restoring my own'. Affronted by the meddling proof-reader, Twain noted that his punctuation was 'none of [the proofreader's] business', and reminded his publishers that he 'knows more about punctuation in two minutes than any damned bastard of a proof-reader can learn in two centuries'. Having satisfied himself that he'd made his point, Twain decided to conserve the rest of his vitriol for another occasion. 'But this is the Sabbath Day,' he closed, '& I must not continue in this worldly vein.' The Sabbath cast a short shadow, however; Twain never went long without a dig at the people fussing with his grammar: 'Yesterday Mr. Hall wrote that the printer's proof-reader was improving my punctuation for me,' he wrote in another letter, '& I telegraphed orders to have him shot without giving him time to pray.'

Twain was aggressive in his criticisms of his proof-readers because he was tuned in to the value of good punctuation.* By 'good', I don't mean what rule books mean by 'good punctuation'. I mean punctuation that is effective, punctuation that is actively making a text better,

---

* In fact, Twain wrote that his punctuation was 'the one thing I am inflexibly particular about … It's got more real variety about it than any other accomplishment I possess, & I reverence it accordingly.' Mark Twain, *Autobiography of Mark Twain, Volume 1: The Complete and Authoritative Edition*, ed. Harriet E. Smith, Benjamin Griffin, Victor Fischer, and Michael Barry Frank (Oakland: University of California Press, 2010), p. 677.

punctuation that is fitted to the tone and style of the text and its purpose. These criteria don't mean that good punctuation won't ever appear to play by The Rules – they just mean it's coincidental if it happens to do so. Punctuation has to be judged by how it shapes the text in which it's situated. The problem, for writers and readers, is how to go about figuring out whether punctuation is any good or not without the security of a book of rules. It's a tough thing to do, to learn to let go of getting answers from style books and to replace that practice with asking exploratory questions about our texts.

I've spent a lot of years talking about punctuation – its history and its modern practices – with people who consider themselves language Learners (often students), and also with people who consider themselves language Masters (usually people who've written a few articles, or a book, or at least a dissertation). I've found that the Masters are the people who are most resistant to the demonstrable truths about rules (the truths you've been reading in this book). The Masters are the people who usually don't really need to refer to the rules in order to use them, and in fact they never needed to memorise the rules in the first place in order to deploy 'proper English'. But they're very certain, nonetheless, that rules are a good thing. These rule lovers possess an innate understanding of the proscriptions provided by rules; they like rules because the rules give words to, and validate, an instinctive understanding of usage that the rule lover already has. Perhaps this rule lover has had to memorise a few of the more obscure rules to possess the complete set in his or her head, but the basics have been there from childhood.

I know this character well, because I *was* that rule lover, that Master. From a young age I could recite *Chicago Manual of Style* precepts by chapter and verse. I got embarrassingly loud hiccups on a school field trip when I was twelve years old because poor grammar on a sign at a national park* offended and shocked my constitution on such a visceral level. I could hear the crack of an infinitive splitting from miles off. Why, *yes*, dear college classmate, I would be *delighted* to proofread that paper for you and hand it back red.

I skipped smugly along in this fashion, straight up until I taught my first class of college students, when I was twenty-three. As soon as I was on the other side of the seminar table standing at a blackboard, my gleeful grammar-nerdery crashed headfirst into a pretty serious pedagogical problem: rules, even when explained very carefully and consistently, didn't seem to be a good way to

---

* An errant apostrophe making an *its* into an *it's*.

teach students what they wanted to know, which was how to have *control and mastery* over language. How do you make words do what you want them to? Rules couldn't answer that question.

Deep down, I think most rule lovers know this. I have yet to meet a rule lover who's been able to tell me that he or she actually learned good English usage by memorising or consulting rules. And even if memorising rules were a good way to learn English successfully, where would knowing and using all the rules with precision actually get you? You could write perfectly 'correct' English all day and still not have what most of us *really* want, which is style. We want our words to have impact. We want our boss to implement that great new idea, we want our texts to inspire love and our tweets to get laughs, we want the eulogy to do justice, we want to sound breezy and cool in that social media profile, we want the A on the paper, we want to persuade and to be understood. Following the rules will not be sufficient to accomplish these things; some of these abilities elude even the people who consider themselves Masters. Maybe the Masters can speak 'standard English' and maybe they can write well enough in obscure jargon and byzantine syntax to be published in some niche academic field, but that might be the *only* English they can speak – and that is a limitation and liability. So what if you know the password to get into the Ivory Tower if you can't get back out of it when you need some fresh air and open sky?

So we need another tactic, whether we think we consider ourselves beginners or advanced. How do we learn to use English in a way that *sticks* better and *works* better than an abstracted list of memorised rules? And how do we learn to develop a writing style that's recognisable, and at the same time master the ability to be flexible with that style as the occasion requires?

I would love to give you a quick fix for this problem. If I could give you a quick fix, I could sell a zillion copies of this book the way that a new diet book promising quick and easy weight loss sells in January. But the results of a quick-fix way to master English would be about as lasting as those of a fad diet. The truth is, it takes more work and more time to become a good English writer than anyone really wants to believe. To write well, you have to read a lot, and you have to read with attention, which is what these next sections will model. You're going to see me stop* and think, *Why did the author choose a semicolon here*

---

* It can be hard to slow ourselves down and really contemplate a piece of text. That's probably always been true, but for me, at least, typing has made it more difficult; when most of my

when she could have chosen a full stop? In some cases, I'm going to look at sentences as parts of paragraphs, which are parts of chapters, which are parts of books: how does this sentence interact with the sentences around it, and how does it create character in fiction or advance an idea or feeling in non-fiction? In other cases, I'll think about the author's overall style or voice or themes: how is the semicolon contributing? Here there will be no contextless 'example sentences' floating in the void. Thinking that you can understand a semicolon by looking at one in a lone example sentence is like thinking you've really seen a lion because you saw one at the local zoo all alone in an enclosure chewing on a T-bone the zookeeper tossed in.

Many of the writers I'll talk about in the following sections have firm opinions about punctuation, or at least

---

writing is done with my fingers flying over a keyboard, I can transcribe an author's words faster than my brain can properly take them in. If I really want to discipline myself and look closely at a writer's style, I still copy out sections of that author's work by hand, pen on paper. I'm a firm believer that this is still the best and most reliable way to learn to be a better stylist, not just when it comes to punctuation, but for the other elements of style as well. I believe this because I've seen it work, over and over, throughout the years. I recommend this technique to anyone who considers themselves to be a student of language, no matter what their age and ability.

they wouldn't disavow punctuation as part of what gives their writing style. Irvine Welsh, however – one of the authors I'll touch on – might not be too impressed with my scrutiny of his semicolons:

> I use [the semicolon]. I've no feelings about it – it's just there. People actually get worked up about that kind of thing, do they? I don't fucking believe it. They should get a fucking life or a proper job. They've got too much time on their hands, to think about nonsense.

Well, them's the breaks if you're a writer. There's an extent to which your analysis of your own work is an interesting jumping-off point for criticism, but there's equally an extent to which your writing is its own entity and exists independent of you and your intentions and your hopes and dreams. Plus, it's entirely possible that a text might have its punctuation altered by a sloppy (or malicious) copy editor; as we've seen in the chapters on the law, transcription and typesetting are vulnerable to human error. Samuel Taylor Coleridge lavished praise on the literary mastery displayed by Daniel Defoe for his use of a semicolon in *Robinson Crusoe* – a semicolon which, it turns out, doesn't appear in the majority of editions of the book. 'In effect,' one critic summed up, 'Coleridge has chosen to praise the work of a typesetter contemporary to himself, not Defoe.' So in terms of exegesis of a book, there are a lot of unknowns that render it hard to know whether we're able to make claims about what an author's intentions really were. Even without certainty about who did what to which part of a text, we can learn by thinking carefully about punctuation in texts. Welsh can claim indeliberate semicoloning all he wants. It doesn't make it less interesting or productive to look at how the semicolon creates narrative voice and meaning in *Trainspotting*.*

THE BIG PAUSE

When we first meet private detective Philip Marlowe in Raymond Chandler's *The Big Sleep*, he is thirty-eight years old and has already seen it all. Marlowe is the consummate noir detective, so hard-boiled that even Diogenes the Cynic might have told him to chill out. In the seven novels and handful of short stories that Chandler wrote featuring Marlowe, semicolons are rare. Often, the world as

---

* Welsh is wrong that thinking about punctuation is 'nonsense', but of course he might nonetheless be right that I need to get a fucking life and a proper job.

Ralph Crane/The LIFE Images Collection/Getty Images

Marlowe describes it tumbles forth with barely any punctuation at all: 'I shaved and showered and dressed and got my raincoat out and went downstairs and looked out of the front door.' Forget the semicolon, we're not even getting *commas*.

A semicolon requires effort and thought to deploy, and as we've seen, some writers avoid them entirely. So you might think, *Maybe Chandler just didn't like the semicolon, or maybe he didn't know how to use one*. But Chandler's essays, sparkling yet far less well known than the Marlowe novels for which he is famous, show otherwise; the essays positively bristle with precisely placed semicolons.

Moreover, Chandler was pernickety about syntax in general, and he wasn't afraid to growl at copy editors who trod too close to what he considered *his* territory. Sitting at his typewriter in January 1947, peering through his horn-rimmed glasses and puffing on his pipe – at least, this is how I picture the scene, because you rarely see a photo of Chandler without a pipe jammed between his lips and a glint in his eye – he fired off a salty letter to his editor at *The Atlantic*, Edward Weeks. 'By the way,' Chandler spat at the end of the letter,

would you convey my compliments to the purist who reads your proofs and tell him or her that I write in a sort of broken-down patois which is something like the way a Swiss waiter talks, and that when I split an infinitive, God damn it, I split it so it will stay split, and when I interrupt the velvety smoothness of my more or less literate syntax with a few sudden words of barroom vernacular, this is done with the eyes wide open and the mind relaxed but attentive. The method may not be perfect, but it is all I have. I think your proofreader is kindly attempting to steady me on my feet, but much as I appreciate the solicitude, I am really able to steer a fairly clear course, provided I get both sidewalks and the street between.

The Atlantic's proofreader, Margaret Mutch, got Chandler's message and wrote him a letter back. This time Chandler responded with a poem, 'Lines to a Lady with an Unsplit Infinitive', in which he imagines confronting Mutch over her correctives. The poem culminates in Mutch murdering Chandler with a crutch:

> His face was white with sudden fright,
> And his syntax lily-livered.

> 'O dear Miss Mutch, leave down your crutch!'
> He cried in thoughtless terror.

> Short shrift she gave. Above his grave:
> HERE LIES A PRINTER'S ERROR.

'Roll on, roll on, thou semicolon,' exhorts Chandler in one line of his impish little poem. And Chandler certainly knew how to let semicolons roll. The *Atlantic* article that prompted his letter and poem was a piece called 'Oscar Night in Hollywood'. There are semicolons aplenty in it, and it has two examples of one of Chandler's most characteristic uses of the semicolon: he loved to pound out a paragraph in which he dressed down someone or something in a series of clauses with more or less identical grammatical form.

If you can go past those awful idiot faces on the bleachers outside the theater without a sense of the collapse of the human intelligence; if you can stand the hailstorm of flash bulbs popping at the poor patient actors who, like kings and queens, have never the right to look bored; if you can glance out over this gathered assemblage of what is supposed to be the elite of Hollywood and say to yourself without a sinking feeling, 'In these hands lie the destinies of the only original art the modern world has conceived'; if you can laugh, and you probably will, at the cast-off jokes from the comedians on the stage, stuff that wasn't good enough to use on their radio shows; if you can stand the fake sentimentality and the platitudes of the officials and the mincing elocution of the glamour queens (you ought to hear them with four martinis down the hatch); if you can do all these things with grace and pleasure, and not have a wild and forsaken horror at the thought that most of these people actually take this shoddy performance seriously; and if you can then go out into the night to see half the police force of Los Angeles gathered to protect the golden ones from the mob in the free seats but not from that awful moaning sound they give out, like destiny whistling through a hollow shell; if you can do all these things and still feel next morning that the picture business is worth the attention of one single intelligent, artistic mind, then in the picture business you certainly belong, because this sort of vulgarity is part of its inevitable price.

The semicolon can be very effective in a paragraph-long sentence like this, where it can highlight and amplify parallel structure. All those clauses in Chandler's list, which begin in the same way ('if you …'), sound like the authoritative repetition of a judge in a courtroom, the semicolon slamming down like a gavel between each indictment and its successor. Here Chandler created a steadiness of rhythm in his prose so that its structure and the words within it work seamlessly to create meaning.*

---

* Possibly this paragraph is also a sly world-weary riff on Rudyard Kipling's inspirational poem 'If', although one would have to ask Chandler to know for sure.

Rhythm is everything for Chandler. Consider one of his other uses of the semicolon in the same 'Oscar Night' essay:

> They insist upon judging it by the picture they saw last week or yesterday; which is even more absurd (in view of the sheer quantity of production) than to judge literature by last week's best-sellers, or the dramatic art by even the best of the current Broadway hits.

Punctuation can let a sentence run or it can hold it in check. Either way the effect can be thrilling. Watch the videos of the great racehorse Secretariat competing for the Triple Crown in 1973. In the Belmont Stakes you see him set free to run seemingly unchecked by his jockey: almost from the first moment of the race it is just Secretariat, Secretariat, Secretariat. He accelerates and accelerates, pulling away until there is only him in the frame when he crosses the finish line. But in the Kentucky Derby, he is held back for most of the race. For a long while he barely figures in the race caller's list of positions. Then suddenly he is let go and is away so quickly and effortlessly he appears to float. Chandler's sentence just quoted is Kentucky Derby-style Secretariat: Chandler reins in that first clause nice and tight and short; and then he lets it go leaping forward, surging with energy and passion felt all the more keenly for the compactness of that first clause. There is a moment of transition between restraint and licence to run, and that moment is made and marked by the semicolon.*

Reading Chandler's essays, there can be no doubt that he knew how to use semicolons and *relished* using them, given their relative frequency in his non-fiction. So why is it that his fiction might contain one or two semicolons, if any at all?† The key, as I hinted at the start of this section, lies in Marlowe's character. Marlowe rarely allows himself either the kind of reflective pause or the uncertainty that a semicolon permits. Marlowe knows what's what. He meets a person and within moments has usually homed in on their innermost self. He's good at chess; he can see clearly several moves ahead. He is unmoved by the blonde hair and sweet smiles of countless femmes fatales. If he makes a mistake, he doesn't spend much (if any) time on

---

* In the late 1800s, incidentally, a racehorse *named* Semicolon did exceptionally well in the major US races, but he began to tire around the turn of the century – much like the semicolon itself.

† I count two in *The Big Sleep*, for instance, and one in *The High Window*.

self-castigation. And perhaps most Marlowe of all is the practice of keeping his cards close to his chest. He is forever getting the players in his investigations drunk and confessional, while confessing nothing himself. Certainly a lot goes on in Marlowe's mind, but Marlowe's mind is quicksilver, all action, few pauses – often there's not even enough time for a comma.

So it is a surprise when Marlowe has a moment of vulnerability midway through *The Big Sleep*.

I didn't mind what she called me, what anybody called me. But this was the room I had to live in. It was all I had in the way of a home. In it was everything that was mine, that had any association for me, any past, anything that took the place of a family. Not much; a few books, pictures, radio, chessmen, old letters, stuff like that. Nothing. Such as they were they had all my memories.

It is a poignant moment. Marlowe reflects on how tenuous is his sense of having any kind of home whatsoever. What takes the place of a family is 'not much' and a short silence. The semicolon reads as Marlowe having to stop to think, perhaps being *made* to stop to think by his sense of loss. For once he seems unguarded. That semicolon could have been a colon or a full stop, but Chandler chose this moment to drop in one of the Marlowe books' rare semicolons.

Both this vulnerable semicolon and the racehorse semicolon we looked at prior to it are 'illegal'. A semicolon, *The Oxford Manual of Style* opines, is to be used either when the items in a list are lengthy and have their own internal punctuation, or when separating two independent or coordinating clauses. Neither criterion applies here: 'which is even more absurd (in view of the sheer quantity of production) than to judge literature by last week's best-sellers, or the dramatic art by even the best of the current Broadway hits' is not an independent clause. Nor does it contain so elaborate a series of punctuation of its own that it could not have been cordoned off with another punctuation mark. The same is true of 'a few books, pictures, radio, chessmen, old letters, stuff like that'.

If you think of Chandler's deployment of these semicolons as 'breaking the rules'; if your first reaction is 'Where the hell is the rest of the sentence?'; if you want to take out your red pen and start correcting; then you have missed the opportunity to feel something more meaningful than irritation. I remember watching those videos of Secretariat's races for the first time as a child. My father had given me a copy of William Nack's book

Secretariat, and I wanted to see for myself the greatness described in its pages. In the Kentucky Derby, when Secretariat was at last set free in the final stretch, I leapt to my feet and shouted. Watching the Belmont Stakes, a chill passed through my body to see such sublime athleticism let loose. Even though those races were run four years before I was born, I had the sense of something alive and unfolding, of momentum and power masterfully reserved and then unfurled, and my reaction to watching them again today, some thirty years later, is the same. Good punctuation, whether it reins in or lets go, can produce the same kinds of exhilarating effects if we aren't unwisely reined in ourselves by a sense that language is somehow obliged to obey a set of rules.

Lynne Truss, our wittiest contemporary rule advocate, cheekily warns that 'weak-charactered writers will be encouraged to ignore the rule that only full sentences should be joined by the semicolon'. Were Truss able to tease Chandler about his 'weak-charactered' writing, I'd like to see what poetry might result from a face-off between the mid-century master of syntax and the modern maven of rules. But Chandler died in 1959. Beneath his name and the dates of his life, his gravestone in San Diego's Mount Hope Cemetery says nothing about a printer's error. It reads, simply, 'Author'.

HEROIN ADDICTS EXPLAIN THINGS TO ME

Are semicolons always pauses, then? Moments of silence? Definitely not. There are other ways to think about the possibilities the semicolon offers a writer. To see some more semicolon tricks, it'll help to look at two writers who don't seem like they belong together: the essayist Rebecca Solnit, and the novelist Irvine Welsh. Solnit's prose is all about clarity, precision, and penetrating intellect, while Welsh spews profanity-laced Scots English in novels like *Trainspotting*, written in the voices of a group of heroin addicts. Radically different in styles, genre, and substance though they may be, Solnit's and Welsh's prose offer an antidote to seeing a semicolon only as a pause longer than a comma or as a precise logical signifier, which are the two most frequently deployed characterisations of the semicolon that you're likely to find. A semicolon is sometimes not a pause, but the opposite: an instrument of quickness, a little springboard that launches you rapidly from thought to thought.

Trainspotting has one of these springy little semicolons in its very first sentence:

The sweat wis lashing oafay Sick Boy; he wis trembling. Ah wis jist sitting thair, focusing oan the telly, tryin no tae notice the cunt. He wis bringing me doon. Ah tried tae keep ma attention oan the Jean-Claude Van Damme video.

This amplification to the news that Sick Boy was sweating, that he was also trembling, has the air of a conspiratorial addendum, the way that good gossip is often quickly whispered. Sick Boy is irritating the narrator of this chapter, Mark Renton, so he talks a little shit about him to us readers.

It's not like the semicolon was Welsh's only option. He could have squealed to a complete halt:

The sweat wis lashing oafay Sick Boy. He wis trembling. Ah wis jist sitting thair, focusing oan the telly, tryin no tae notice the cunt. He wis bringing me doon. Ah tried tae keep ma attention oan the Jean-Claude Van Damme video.

Instead, Welsh uses the semicolon to create energy and the kind of molten realism characteristic of his caustic prose. Renton's voice has much more texture and life for having three different punctuation marks playing off one another in this paragraph than it would with only commas and full stops.

It seems Welsh is fond of this strategy for opening lines, and who can blame him? For Welsh's books it works well to make his readers feel dropped into a racing river, swept into the action from the first moment. Welsh's opening paragraph in 'A Soft Touch' makes use of the same type of quick semicolon: 'It wis good fir a while wi Katrina, but she did wrong by me. And that's no jist something ye can forget; no jist like that.'

Rebecca Solnit, too, deploys semicolons that speed things up rather than slowing them down. In her essay 'Diary', she reflects on the changes wrought by modern technology, and reminisces about a pre-1995 world: 'That bygone time had rhythm, and it had room for you to do one thing at a time; it had different parts; mornings included this, and evenings that, and a great many of us had these schedules in common.' The effect is like a stone skipping across water, lightly touching it three times, just for a split second, before hopping on. Think about how different this sentence would be if Solnit had chosen to put a colon either after *time* or after *parts*, as she very well could have. That sentence would seem comparatively heavy and academic. The quick-skip lightness of Solnit's semicolons, by contrast, has a pleasing breeziness that suits her nostalgic attitude towards the bygone time she describes.

Solnit seems to like semicolon duos and trios, and they are usually fleet-footed semicolons like the ones just quoted, but they enact a subtler kind of speeding-up as well. Have a look at these semicolon sequences each of which fires off data supporting Solnit's central argument:

Instead, we hear that American men commit murder-suicides – at the rate of about twelve a week – because the economy is bad, though they also do it when the economy is good; or that those men in India murdered the bus rider because the poor resent the rich, while other rapes in India are explained by how the rich exploit the poor; and then there are those ever-popular explanations: mental problems and intoxicants – and for jocks, head injuries.

Of course, women are capable of all sorts of major unpleasantness, and there are violent crimes by women, but the so-called war of the sexes is extraordinarily lopsided when it comes to actual violence. Unlike the last (male) head of the International Monetary Fund, the current (female) head is not going to assault an employee at a luxury hotel; top-ranking female officers in the US military, unlike their male counterparts, are not accused of any sexual assaults; and young female athletes, unlike those male football players in Steubenville, aren't likely to urinate on unconscious boys, let alone violate them and boast about it in YouTube videos and Twitter feeds.

Good things came about with the new technologies. Many people now have voices without censorship; many of us can get in touch with other ordinary citizens directly, through every new medium, from blogs to tweets to texts to posts on FB and Instagram. In 1989, Tiananmen Square was the fax revolution. Email helped organize the Seattle WTO shutdown in 1999; Facebook was instrumental in the Arab Spring's initial phase in 2011; Occupy Wall Street was originally a Twitter hashtag.

We readers leap from fact to fact, but I would lay down a decent chunk of change that Solnit didn't. Each of these facts and figures required research, possibly even several hours of research in order to dig up a relevant statistic, verify that the methodology that produced it was sound, and survey any competing data that might challenge its veracity.*

A great essay is like a great nature show. Sir David Attenborough, his plummy voice suddenly sharp with excitement, narrates a dramatic chase scene on Fernandina Island in the Galápagos. Fernandina is a foreboding volcanic landscape that's home to over seven thousand seafaring marine iguanas, which can hold their breath up to half an hour as they dive and graze the sea grasses. A newly hatched marine iguana cautiously lifts his head out of the island's pebbly substrate, just enough to roll one bright little eye around his surroundings. Almost as soon as he decides it's safe to emerge, dozens of racer snakes dart from the shadows of the rocks. The iguana seems almost impossibly light on his brand-new feet, but there are too many snakes, hordes and hordes of them spilling out from under every overhang, and soon the iguana has disappeared into a greedy knot of them. The same fate befalls a second tiny iguana. And it seems a third is

---

* The problem is magnified in historical narrative non-fiction. The labour that can go into summoning the atmosphere of another era is boggling – a historian might spend hours poring over old newspapers to find out how hot some particular day was, just for half a sentence adding colour to the past.

destined for the same gruesome end … but this one improbably slips free, soaring to safety on the rocks near the shore as one last racer snake flails his fangs at the iguana's heels. The entire chase sequence lasts less than six minutes. But a few minutes of what is 'wild' and 'natural' in these shows takes hundreds of hours of filming to achieve: the *Planet Earth* crew staked out the iguanas' hatching ground dawn to dusk for two weeks to gather footage. Indeed, the hour-long 'Islands' episode as a whole required three and a half years to plan, shoot, and produce – all to give us a glimpse of business as usual in the natural world.

Likewise, a really great essay puts on display the seemingly natural movement of the author's thoughts which, in reality, required supernatural effort and umpteen takes to collect and edit. 'Remember that writing is not typing,' Solnit advises. 'Thinking, researching, contemplating, outlining, composing in your head and in sketches, maybe some typing with revisions as you go and then more revisions, emendations, additions, reflections, setting aside and returning afresh, because a good writer is always a good editor of his or her work.' Reading a good essay is a bit like watching a well-edited nature show. It gives the illusion of thought spilling naturally and fluidly onto the page. In Solnit's case, semicolons are quick cuts keeping things exciting and saving the reader from the sense of labour and drudgery that the author herself no doubt expended.

Having managed to run the gauntlet of racer snakes, the baby marine iguana is in position to make his first dive into the sea, where he'll swim deftly through the currents to nip at a green carpet of plants. Now we, too, dive into the sea, in search of more semicolons.

BLUBBER AND BLATHER

At the time of Herman Melville's death in 1891, his novel *Moby-Dick* had sold only a few thousand copies. When the book's publishing house burned down in 1853, two years after publication, there were still first-run copies of it stacked in the warehouse, feeding the flames. Melville spent much of his working life as a customs inspector after finally throwing in the towel on writing.

No doubt the generally negative reviews that *Moby-Dick* received contributed to its floundering in bookshops. Its thick and thorny prose clambered down one page and onto the next in long paragraphs studded with every word between the covers of *Webster's*, plus a few more that Melville had invented for the book. One reviewer, having managed to slash through this thicket and come out the other side of the novel alive but not unscathed, minced no words of his own in concluding his testy review: 'But if there are any of our readers who wish to find examples of bad rhetoric, involved syntax, stilted sentiment and incoherent English, we will take the liberty of recommending to them this precious volume of Mr Melville's.' He was not alone in his assessment: most reviewers seemed perplexed and frequently infuriated by Melville's elliptical, meandering prose. 'The style of his tale is in places disfigured by mad (rather than bad) English,' lamented a critic for the *London Athenaeum*.

Some of the book's madness undoubtedly stems from its conceit as a dodgy draft of a true story. *Moby-Dick* is told in the first person. Some (maybe most) first-person books are just told from within the narrator's perspective without being *conceptualised* as books. *Moby-Dick* is different. It's presented as Ishmael's written account of his days on the *Pequod*, the whaling ship that sets out in pursuit of the infamous white whale. This book, the product of his education at sea, might prove the only good and profitable thing he's ever done.

And, as for me, if, by any possibility, there be any as yet undiscovered prime thing in me; if I shall ever deserve any real repute in that small but high hushed world which I might not be unreasonably ambitious of; if hereafter I shall do anything that, upon the whole, a man might rather have done than to have left undone; if, at my death, my executors, or more properly my creditors, find any precious MSS. in my desk, then here I prospectively ascribe all the honour and the glory to whaling; for a whale-ship was my Yale College and my Harvard.

Not only is *Moby-Dick* self-consciously Ishmael's book, it's a *draft* of a book – at least, to the extent that Ishmael is aware how much is left necessarily unfinished in it. Near the end of his catalogue of whales, he adds a little apologia:

Finally: It was stated at the outset, that this system would not be here, and at once, perfected. You cannot but plainly see that I have kept my word. But I now leave my cetological System standing thus unfinished, even as the great Cathedral of Cologne was left, with the crane still standing upon the top of the uncompleted tower. For small erections may be finished by their first architects; grand ones, true ones, ever leave the copestone to posterity. God keep me from ever completing anything. This whole book is but a draught – nay, but the draught of a draught. Oh, Time, Strength, Cash, and Patience!

At least one modern fan of *Moby-Dick* acknowledges this aspect of the text as part of its beauty and magic: 'But "Moby-Dick" is not a novel. It's barely a book at all,' wrote Philip Hoare in the *New Yorker*. 'It's more an act of transference, of ideas and evocations hung around the vast and unknowable shape of the whale, an extended musing on the strange meeting of human history and natural history.' These 'ideas and evocations' that are 'hung around' the whale are held in suspension by the book's four-thousand-odd semicolons, sturdy little nails holding narrative thread spread out wide enough to comprehend not just a whale but everything the whale comes to mean to the men hunting it.

When it comes to plot, the book isn't really all that. 'The plot is meagre beyond comparison, as the whole of the incident might very conveniently have been comprised in half of one of these three interminable volumes,' complained a reviewer for the *London Britannia*; many modern readers have felt the same way.* The truly great moments in the book come when Ishmael goes off on what could be considered a tangent. There are entire chapters devoted to whale fat, or to the colour white, or to questions about whether the whale has shrunk since God first created it. At the paragraph level, too, Ishmael is prone to wandering off.

It's true that Melville isn't afraid of a long sentence, but I've seen longer sentences. (Ask me about my Faulkner phase.) No, it's not really that Melville uses the semicolon to stretch out the distance between a capital letter and a full stop; instead, the semicolons are in the service of carrying you slowly, gently, pleasurably away from whatever it was you thought you were reading about – the process of decapitating a whale, or how to assess winds, or cannibalism.

I say 'pleasurably', but of course some people don't find these digressions pleasurable at all, and would have

---

* One of my favourite college professors was an ex-lawyer who retained an attorney's prose sensibility when reading essays. Any superfluous or vague adjective was excised, leaving a red looping line with 'DOES NO WORK' written neatly beside the wound. I sometimes wonder what *Moby-Dick* might look like if he had dug into the heap of adjectives and adverbs sitting atop nearly every noun and verb.

agreed with Melville's contemporary critics, not our present-day appraisal of the book, which counts it among the best of American novels. After it was rediscovered by literary critics in the 1920s, Melville's flop was transformed into a classic. The *Guardian*'s list of the best 100 English-language books ever written called it 'wise, funny, and gripping'. Readers now pick it up based on its literary repute or because it's a requirement for a class, and after a few pages many of those readers would gladly hurl it into the depths. Even when the action picks up, Ishmael's narration isn't exactly economical. He often uses semicolons to string several events into sequence:

> When instantly, the entire ship careens over on her side; every bolt in her starts like the nail-heads of an old house in frosty weather; she trembles, quivers, and nods her frightened mast-heads to the sky. More and more she leans over to the whale, while every gasping heave of the windlass is answered by a helping heave from the billows; till at last, a swift, startling snap is heard; with a great swash the ship rolls upward and backward from the whale, and the triumphant tackle rises into sight dragging after it the disengaged semi-circular end of the first strip of blubber.

Even his *jokes* require extended set-ups that sometimes take the text wandering off from the matter at hand (and the matter at hand is, as always, more likely than not to be tangential to the 'main events' of the book already):

In the case of a small Sperm Whale the brains are accounted a fine dish. The casket of the skull is broken into with an axe, and the two plump, whitish lobes being withdrawn (precisely resembling two large puddings), they are then mixed with flour, and cooked into a most delectable mess, in flavor somewhat resembling calf's head, which is quite a dish among some epicures; and everyone knows that some young bucks among the epicures, by continually dining upon calves' brains, by and by get to have a little brains of their own, so as to be able to tell a calf's head from their own heads; which, indeed, requires uncommon discrimination. And that is the reason why a young buck with an intelligent-looking calf's head before him, is somehow one of the saddest sights you can see. The head looks a sort of reproachfully at him, with an 'Et tu, Brute!' expression.

But wait – we were supposed to be talking about eating *whales* ...

'Its oceanic reach and perverse digression provide endless sources of inspiration and interpretation,' writes Philip Hoare. 'In chapters such as the famously sublime "The Whiteness of the Whale" – almost hallucinatory in its associative suspension of normality and subtle obscenity – Melville takes up his theme, then takes it apart, teasing it out to impossibly filigreed tendrils, until you wonder how you, or he, got there in the first place.' Eventually Melville's disquisition on the idea of whiteness winds its way back to the matter of hunting Moby-Dick, but only after sideswiping practically every subject in the arts and sciences:

> Is it that by its indefiniteness it shadows forth the heartless voids and immensities of the universe, and thus stabs us from behind with the thought of annihilation, when beholding the white depths of the milky way? Or is it, that as in essence whiteness is not so much a color as the visible absence of color, and at the same time the concrete of all colors; is it for these reasons that there is such a dumb blankness, full of meaning, in a wide landscape of snows – a colorless, all-color of atheism

from which we shrink? And when we consider that other theory of the natural philosophers, that all other earthly hues – every stately or lovely emblazoning – the sweet tinges of sunset skies and woods; yea, and the gilded velvets of butterflies, and the butterfly cheeks of young girls; all these are but subtile deceits, not actually inherent in substances, but only laid on from without; so that all deified Nature absolutely paints like the harlot, whose allurements cover nothing but the charnel-house within; and when we proceed further, and consider that the mystical cosmetic which produces every one of her hues, the great principle of light, for ever remains white or colorless in itself, and if operating without medium upon matter, would touch all objects, even tulips and roses, with its own blank tinge – pondering all this, the palsied universe lies before us a leper; and like wilful travellers in Lapland, who refuse to wear colored and coloring glasses upon their eyes, so the wretched infidel gazes himself blind at the monumental white shroud that wraps all the prospect around him. And of all these things the Albino Whale was the symbol. Wonder ye then at the fiery hunt?

The semicolon was the perfect punctuation mark for capturing the 'mystical and well nigh ineffable' 'horror' occasioned by the whiteness of the whale, which Ishmael 'almost despair[ed] of putting in a comprehensible form'.

Some readers thought Ishmael's despair was well justified. Suggestive and beautiful though Melville's disquisition on the whale's whiteness may be to many readers (myself included), it confounded and repelled others, especially those who picked up a copy of *Moby-Dick* after devouring one of Melville's previous novels. He didn't start out his literary career with the penumbral writing style that fogged the plot of *Moby-Dick*. His first novel, *Typee*, was a bestselling account of two sailors' adventures in Polynesia. Many critics longed to return to those islands. 'Mr. Melville grows wilder and more

Bones of the right whale, from Recent Memoirs on the Cetacea (1866)

untamable with every adventure,' a review in the *New York Evangelist* observed. 'In *Typee* and *Omoo*, he began with a semblance of life and reality, though it was often but the faintest kind of semblance. As he advanced, he threw off the pretence of probability, and wandered into the mist and vagueness of poetry and fantasy, and now in this last venture, has reached the very limbo of eccentricity.'* *Typee*, with its 'semblance of reality', had less use for the semicolon (although to be sure, Melville still exercised it plenty). The novel clocked in at around 107,000 words and 845 semicolons, a rate of approximately one semicolon for every 127 words. *Moby-Dick*, on the other hand, was about double the length at around 210,000 words, but had *4,000* semicolons. That's one for every 52 words. The semicolons are *Moby-Dick*'s joints, allowing the novel the freedom of movement it needed to tour such a large and disparate collection of themes.

D. H. Lawrence, who helped dredge Melville back up from obscurity in the 1920s, wrote of *Moby-Dick* that 'there is something really overwhelming in these

---

* The reviewer meant 'limbo' as in a place of oblivion, but for the modern reader more familiar with the West Indies dance, the idea of Melville bending over backwards to scoot under an ever-lowering bar of literary decency works just as well to capture this critic's opinion.

whale-hunts, almost superhuman or inhuman, bigger than life, more terrific than human activity'. In its narrative structure and ambition as well as its themes, *Moby-Dick* was ahead of its time, in uncharted waters. Just as sailors needed instruments to wander out past sight of shore, *Moby-Dick* required writing technologies that could allow it to venture out beyond the genre constraints of its time, and one of those technological marvels – as slender and significant as a compass needle – was the semicolon.

TRUST ME, I'M A WRITER

Looking at me over the rim of a teacup on a rainy London afternoon, my friend Suzanne chooses her words carefully. 'We don't really think of him as a popular writer,' she says diplomatically, in response to my announcement that I'm working on a section on Henry James's semicolons. We Americans* don't think of him as a popular writer either, I assure her.

---

* Many Americans are surprised to learn Henry James is one of their own; they often think he was British. James wanted readers not to be able to tell whether he was American or British, and among his own people, he seems to have got his way. I'm curious whether he can hoodwink Brits in a similar fashion.

If reviews for *Moby-Dick* ranged from lukewarm to cool, reviews for Henry James's later work were often ice cold. His books produced 'acute periodic exasperation' in their readers. His sentences were 'cumbrous and difficult, struggling through a press of hints and ideas'. A review of his 1904 book, *The Golden Bowl*, appeared under the heading 'A Novel for the Select Few'. The reviewer wagered that 'a more difficult book to read surely was never written. It is the minutest study in the psychological analysis of certain highly complex, over-refined, over-sensitised present-day persons.' For casual readers, the book was 'unreadable', and anyone with any kind of a life beyond sprawling on a chaise longue had better not even try: 'Life is too short to master its intricacies of style and treatment.' Or, as another, more circumspect reviewer tactfully put it, the book was to be recommended only for 'the seasoned reader of Henry James'.*

Melville, at least, was allowed to fade quietly back into an ordinary life. Henry James had no such luck, in part because of his famous older brother, William. William

---

* Modern reader 'Sandra', reviewing *The Portrait of a Lady* on Amazon UK, has an apt diagnosis to offer: 'Author just likes to write, almost anything than get to the crux of the story.' She gave it one star.

James, psychologist and philosopher, was beloved by the public. He thrived in front of a crowd; Henry, on the other hand, declined to give interviews and eventually holed up in quiet Sussex. Like so many younger brothers, Henry was destined to be compared to his older sibling whether he liked it or not. The long shadow William's accomplishments cast didn't offer much in the way of flattering lighting for Henry:

> Someone has said that 'Henry James is a novelist who writes like a psychologist and William James a psychologist who writes like a novelist.' The epigram pays the greater compliment to the psychologist for it is much more difficult for a man of science to write charmingly of his speciality than for a literary man to acquire mannerism and become obscure. Certain it is that William James is the most popular of philosophers and Henry James not impossibly the least popular of novelists.

In his sixties, facing down a lifetime of mixed reviews, Henry went back through his early novels and stories and created revised versions of them. These heavily altered stories were published by Scribner between 1907 and

1909 and are known as the 'New York Editions'. James's revisions shone harsh introspective light into previously shadowy corners of his characters' minds, exploding sentence after sentence with laborious psychological detail. The revisions are perplexing; suddenly, there is little space for the reader's imagination or inference. Every thought is so painstakingly spelled out, every object so slavishly described, that the atmosphere of the book becomes suffocating. Nothing is left unsaid.

Sentences puffed out in this way become difficult even to comprehend. Watch how the directness of a sentence in James's 1877 edition of his novel *Roderick Hudson* becomes tortured and effortful. The original version was no short sentence, but it was well managed:

> She was a woman for the light, not for the shade; and her natural line was not picturesque reserve and mysterious melancholy, but frank, joyous, brilliant action, with just so much meditation as was necessary, and not a grain more.

Revised, its punctuation barely holds it together: phrases come rushing like water through the barriers of colons and commas and semicolons.

She was a creature for the sun and the air, for no sort of hereditary shade or equivocal gloom; and her natural line was neither imposed reserve nor mysterious melancholy, but positive life, the life of the great world – his great world – not the *grand monde* as there understood if he wasn't mistaken, which seemed squeezable into a couple of rooms of that inconvenient and ill-warmed house: all with nothing worse to brood about, when necessary, than the mystery perhaps of the happiness that would so queerly have come to her.

'You can never revise too often!' I used to tell students, before I had read much James.

One of the starkest differences generated by James's revisions can be glimpsed in a climactic scene near the end of *Portrait of a Lady*. Isabel Archer, the protagonist, has been tricked into marrying Gilbert Osmond, who schemes with his ex-lover Madame Merle to poach the extraordinary fortune Isabel has inherited. After discovering Osmond's deception, Isabel finds herself alone with an admirer she had once rejected, Caspar Goodwood. In the original 1881 edition of the novel, James's account of what passes between Isabel and Goodwood is oblique, restrained, and allows the simile of 'lightning' maximum impact. 'He glared at her a moment through the dusk, and the next instant she felt his arms about her and his lips on her own lips. His kiss was like a flash of lightning; when it was dark again she was free.' Why on earth did James need to tinker with this perfect set of sentences? But tinker he did.

> His kiss was like white lightning, a flash that spread, and spread again, and stayed; and it was extraordinarily as if, while she took it, she felt each thing in his hard manhood that had least pleased her, each aggressive fact of his face, his figure, his presence, justified of its intense identity and made one with this act of possession. So had she heard of those wrecked and under water following a train of images before they sink. But when darkness returned she was free.

It's not that the revision makes for an *awful* passage. It's just that compared to the original, it feels so heavy-handed. Looking at the grammar of the original version of the sentence, I picture Gale Sondergaard as Mrs Hammond in the noir cinema classic *The Letter*, hovering behind a beaded curtain in a glittering dress. The semicolon is that tantalising veil shimmering between the two halves of the sentence, showing us just enough to let us dream.

In the revised version of the passage, on the other hand, the semicolon makes me think of Sisyphus. The semicolon is a shoulder pressed against the heaviness of the back half of the sentence, trying desperately to huff its weight forwards so that ... well, I'm not sure, exactly. But wherever James is going with the sentence, that semicolon is straining just to keep the whole thing from collapsing on itself. More significant even than the shift in style is the loss of a potently poetic irony. In the revised version, we lose the beautifully ominous paradox of the proximity of the flash of lightning, the spark of passion that traps Isabel, to the freedom that comes when that bright light is extinguished. The attraction that Isabel feels to Goodwood is a different type of constraint than her marriage to Osmond, but it is, nonetheless, a loss of freedom in which she does not act but is acted upon; when the light vanishes and she is 'free', she runs.

In the passages he went back and painstakingly altered, James's modifications feel anxious, as though he were nervous we readers just couldn't be trusted with the freedom of the first version. What might we imagine, what might we feel? Better not to leave it up to us, he seems to have decided. Not only did he bloat sentences throughout the book with a map of Isabel's every thought, he changed the ending of the novel, removing any ambiguity as to whether Isabel might reject Osmond and choose Goodwood instead, or even reject them both and strike out on her own. In the revised version, he made it as clear as he could that Isabel returned to Osmond. There is no other choice for us to consider. And so he closed the gaps, sweeping away the vague.

On the other hand, Henry's famous older brother not only allowed for vagueness, he celebrated it. 'It is in short, the reinstatement of the vague and inarticulate to its proper place in our mental life which I am so anxious to press on the attention,' he wrote in his magnum opus, *The Principles of Psychology*. So often we think it is the business of science always to be exact, but William James had rather the opposite idea when he set about founding the Psychology Department at Harvard. 'The boundary line of the mental is certainly vague,' he urged.

It is better not to be pedantic, but to let the science be as vague as its subject, and include such phenomena as these if by so doing we can throw any light on the main business at hand ... At a certain stage in the development of every science a degree of vagueness is what best consists with fertility.

William searched for ways to unfold possibility in his writing. 'Use the word "field" here for "datum" – it is conveniently ambiguous,' he corrected himself in the margins of lecture notes. He used 'vague' as a compliment when evaluating psychological terminology like 'idea'. William's revisions opened windows; Henry's revisions slammed doors.

The semicolon, as the first version of Isabel Archer and Caspar Goodwood's kiss shows, can certainly support vagueness. Indeed, that's one of the charges levelled at it by semicolon hater Professor Robinson. The semicolon, Paul Robinson contends, is frequently 'used to gloss over an imprecise thought'. Semicolons, he goes on, 'place two clauses in some kind of relation to one another but relieve the writer of saying exactly what that relation is'.*

Poetic omissions of the type Henry James produced at his best would certainly fall into the category of

---

* It is true that the semicolon can be used to cover up sloppy reasoning, but that scarcely seems to be a problem inherent in, or exclusive to, that particular punctuation mark. You want to see some imprecise thoughts? I can manufacture some for you, with naught but a handful of words and maybe a full stop. Nonetheless, the glossings-over that often accompany the semicolons Robinson encounters (he refers in particular to student essays) generate a sense of repulsion in him, and he himself eschews the mark wherever possible.

'imprecise thoughts'. A lot of people, not just Robinson, find an imprecise thought uncomfortable: to these types, it looks like a leak to plug rather than an opportunity to let thoughts flow. Some of those leak-pluggers end up clogging up the works professionally, by becoming analytic philosophers. The analytic philosopher (there are other types of philosophers – or, as I usually think of them, other lunch-table cliques in philosophy) thinks of himself as clear, objective, and precise, and loves to start sentences with phrases like *It is obvious* … or *It is clear that* … Vagueness, especially *deliberate* vagueness, is apt to cause these types to hyperventilate. In spite of this, analytic philosophers consider a master of strategic vaguery, Ludwig Wittgenstein, one of their founding fathers. Wittgenstein sometimes wrote in aphorisms, and even those who claim him as part of the analytic camp admit he was 'exotic' and had a writing style that 'transcends the limits of academic philosophy'. Occasionally, the temptation to try to iron out Wittgenstein's ambiguities and bring him in line with more status-quo philosophical writing became overwhelming for his translators, many of whom were coming from the analytic camp themselves. Check out what G. E. M. Anscombe perpetrates when she translates this fantastically vague semicolon from Wittgenstein's German into English. Here's the original:

Der Philosoph behandelt eine Frage; wie eine Krankheit.

Which you *could* translate so as to preserve the ambiguity in it:

The philosopher treats a question; like an illness.

But Anscombe renders it:

The philosopher's treatment of a question is like the treatment of an illness.

What a different sentence that is. Gone is what German philosophy expert Erich Heller called a 'profound' semicolon, a semicolon that 'marks a frontier between a thought and a triviality'. Could Anscombe just not stand the uncertainty in it, and the multiple possible meanings that that uncertainty permits? I guess the analytic philosopher treats ambiguity; like an illness.*

---

* Although I'm not a fan of Anscombe's imposing her own yen for systematisation and certainty on Wittgenstein here, let no one think Anscombe wasn't a badass. A dazzling and powerful thinker whose extraordinary abilities were acknowledged even in the boys' club of mid-1900s philosophy, she took no shit

Henry James, at his best, *could* stand uncertainties. So often his early writing explored what is only imagined or hinted at between two people. Of the first version of *Portrait of a Lady*, one of James's reviewers wrote: 'As a rule Mr James rejects symphonies, and attempts no harmonising conclusions. He leaves us usually tantalised, half angry with an end which is left to our imagination.' That was precisely his strength. Of the Tartarean options, I definitely prefer Tantalising ambiguities to Sisyphean semicolons.

But that reviewer of James is correct that uncertainty, ambiguity, and vagueness do put a certain burden on the reader. Or maybe it's better to say: they highlight the fact that writing is an exchange between at least two people: writer and reader, or sometimes writer and the writer's own future self. There is nothing wrong with trying to be as precise as possible in your writing, or with trying to be clear; those goals are often productive and have their place. But I don't think it's such a bad thing sometimes to

---

from anyone. Once, in Boston, she attempted to enter a formal restaurant wearing trousers. When told ladies were not allowed to enter in trousers, she simply whipped them off and walked on in. See Jane O'Grady, 'Elizabeth Anscombe: an exhilarating philosopher, she took to sporting a monocle and smoking cigars', *Guardian* (10 January 2001).

be engaged in the practice of working things out in words, of having a conversation. Ambiguity can be useful and productive, and it can make some room for new ideas. It can help the reader *create* something out of the materials the writer provides. As we've seen in Chapters Four and Five, even writing meant to be crystal clear contains points that can be argued, so it's worth thinking constructively about what productive possibilities ambiguity allows and how we can tell when an ambiguity is useful, rather than just pretending we can eliminate it if we only try hard enough.

Ambiguity can be so unsettling in part because when it comes down to it, all writing is an act of trust. As a reader, you trust a writer to give you some pay-off for your efforts. You trust the writer to be telling you the truth, or trying. In turn, as a writer – of an email, a letter, a tweet, a book – you hope that your reader will be generous in interpreting your words. You hope you'll be taken seriously when you want to be. You hope to be understood. Trying to eliminate ambiguity (however doomed a task that is) can at least soothe that anxiety a bit. But art that allows the imagination to participate in it – the kind of art Henry James's early novels displayed – is a beautiful testament to the value that can lie in ambiguity. Uncertainty, after all, is very human, and can call forth our best human virtues. 'If you'll only trust me, how little you will be disappointed!' Goodwood says to Isabel, a line that James left unrevised in *Portrait of a Lady*. If only you'd trust us readers, Henry, how little you might be disappointed too.

THE LINE AND THE DASH: WHY USE THE SEMICOLON NOW?

Perhaps because of the persistent criticism his novels faced, Henry James did not give interviews. His reticence was well known, and so it was a surprise and delight for a journalist from the *New York Times* to be granted the opportunity to conduct James's very first interview in 1915, when he was seventy-one years old. James was prodded out of his silence by his desire to make public the charitable work of the American Volunteer Motor Ambulance Corps. Anxious to make certain his thoughts were represented properly, James spoke 'with much consideration' and asked that 'his punctuation as well as his words should be noted'. Perhaps emboldened by James's having raised the topic himself, the interviewer broke from the designated topic of the discussion mid-interview. 'Are you not famous, Mr. James,' he asked, 'for the use of dashes?' The response was sharp and swift.

'Dash my fame!' he impatiently replied. 'And remember, please, that dogmatizing about punctuation is exactly as foolish as dogmatizing about any other form of communication with the reader. All such forms depend on the kind of thing one is doing and the kind of effect one intends to produce. Dashes, it seems almost platitudinous to say, have their particular representative virtue, their quickening face, and, to put it roughly, strike both the familiar and the empathic note, when those are the notes required, with a felicity beyond either the comma or the semicolon; although indeed a fine sense of the semicolon, like any sort of sense at all for the pluperfect tense and the subjunctive mood, on which the whole perspective in a sentence may depend, seems anything but common.'

Today it's hard to imagine an author being famous for dashes, as Henry James was. In his work, the dash – cutting a path through almost any page you turn to – is like a vector arrow charting the swift forward trajectory of a character's thoughts, or sometimes just the opposite – an arm outstretched as a barrier to keep one thought from tumbling into the next, so quickly do they spill out on the page. In his private letters, the dash was conscripted to signal a change of topic the way we might use a paragraph indent. James's multipurpose use of the dash now looks remarkably modern, but he certainly didn't use it reflexively out of lack of thinking through the options, the way many of us are guilty of deploying it today. It's too bad, really: the dash can be brilliant. The electrifying German Romantic writer Heinrich von Kleist used the dash in his 1808 short story 'Die Marquise von O …' to capture the forgotten space of time during which the unconscious Marquise is raped. It is a masterpiece of mimesis and ironic understatement. Nearly every line of Emily Dickinson's later poetry is sliced with a dash or two. Nicholson Baker was fond of a dash followed by a comma, a hybrid mark he dubbed 'the dashtard'. All these uses of the dash represented deliberation and careful choice.

But the dash nowadays is the Punctuation Mark of First Resort, able to take the place of commas, colons, semicolons, and full stops. We now live in the Era of the Dash. Dashes are dashed off right and left by millions of thumbs sweeping fleetly across millions of mobile phones. A couple of years ago I gave up using the dash for Lent*

---

* I haven't got a religious bone in my body, but I enjoy the Lenten ritual of challenging oneself with deprivation of some kind.

when I noticed a page of my writing was downright staticky with horizontal lines. I wore out my backspace key sticking to my resolution. The dash is so easy, so quick, and – when deployed in the way it often is now – so conveniently empty of meaning.

It's easy enough to blame all of this on the evils of technology, and to act as though the world is fundamentally changing, fracturing, and getting worse; in that reading of reality, the homogenising force of the dash is a symptom of this larger decline. In convincing ourselves of this, we march backwards in the footsteps of our ancestors. Thoreau built his cabin alone on Walden Pond to 'live deep' away from the buzzing city over 150 years ago. The world has always seemed too noisy and too quick. It's worth remembering that for all the things that have capsized in the wake of technological progress, there are new pleasures too: long-lost friends rediscovered through a Google search; online communities coalescing around every obscure interest imaginable; the ability to read books in completely new ways solely through having the tools to search them efficiently; devices with which to call an ambulance or look up the Heimlich manoeuvre quickly.

Still, technology takes even while it gives, and it's not unreasonable to feel that one of the things it is taking is our ability to stop occasionally, or at least to slow down. We bob along feeling helpless on a frantic current of light and noise, always on the move, our predicament best depicted in the linear leap forwards of the dash. The semicolon represents a way to slow down, to stop,* and to think; it measures time more meditatively than the catch-all dash, and it can't be chucked thoughtlessly into just any sentence in place of just any other mark. Even a semicolon that creates a quickness in prose, like the type Rebecca Solnit often uses, requires time and thought to orchestrate. Semicoloned sentences cannot be dashed off.

Back in the city, writing up the lessons he had learned away from 'civilization', Thoreau praised a life lived in the present:

> In any weather, at any hour of the day or night, I have been anxious to improve the nick of time, and notch it on my stick too; to stand on the meeting of two eternities, the past and future, which is precisely the present moment; to toe that line.

---

* A stop without stopping completely. Who wants the full stop right now, with its silence and finality like a red button pressed, or a clock striking midnight?

As we learn to contend with the technologies of the present moment and look for space in which to feel we, too, are really *present*, not pitched helplessly into the future or anchored to the past, we might find it good to look more often to a much older technology, the semicolon, notched into our sentences; to toe that line.

VIII

PERSUASION AND PRETENSION

Are Semicolons for Snobs?

The claim that the semicolon harbours nefarious ambiguities isn't the only accusation it's been dogged by. People also think semicolons are for highfalutin snobs. Paul Robinson calls them 'pretentious'. June Casagrande, who writes on language for the *Los Angeles Times*, declares that semicolons are 'favored by writers who are so proud they know how to use semicolons that they'll happily short-change readers to show off their knowledge'.

Allegations that the semicolon is pretentious have grown increasingly common in the last few decades, but they date back at least to the late nineteenth century, when one commentator celebrated the 'elitist' character of the semicolon that so disgusts Robinson and galls Casagrande:

> It seems paradoxical to assert that the simplest method of isolating the masters of modern English literature is carefully to observe the frequency and propriety of their semicolons; and yet, like the Oxford college where the fellows were chosen by the grace with which they were able to dispose of the stones from the plum tart, the semicolon test may prove the final one to determine the author's fitness to rank with august society.

I would no more argue for measuring the intelligence of a person with their use of semicolons than with their ability to finesse plum pits out of tarts; but neither do I hold with obliterating the semicolon, any more than I would refuse to eat a slice of plum tart just because someone somewhere associates them with snobbery. There is no need to hate semicolons without let, or love commas unequivocally: you can react passionately towards individual instances of their usage without having to swear allegiance to, or vendettas against, the marks themselves.

The semicolon has sometimes been associated with elitism, but it certainly doesn't need to be that way. We've already seen Irvine Welsh use it in Scots dialect in the previous chapter, and not because he's trying to make his characters sound like they went to Eton and are internationally ranked in dressage. And a whole host of other writers who venture outside the confines of formal English use semicolons too. They are everywhere in Junot Díaz's *The Brief Wondrous Life of Oscar Wao*, told from the point of view of the title character's friend Yunior in his Dominican-American patois. Charles Chesnutt's 'Po' Sandy' captures ex-slave Uncle Julius's speech rhythms with semicolons. It seems to me it's not justifiable either to praise or to punish the semicolon as a snob's mark.

The semicolon has, furthermore, been drafted in the fight for equality. The finest deployment of semicolons I've ever come across, in fact, is in Martin Luther King, Jr's 'Letter from Birmingham Jail', which King wrote longhand in the margins of a newspaper while imprisoned in Alabama for civil disobedience. The letter defends King's agitation for civil rights against fellow clergymen who felt he should show more patience. The passage from the letter that contains the remarkable semicolons is a long one, and I suggest reading it out loud to really feel their effects.

Perhaps it is easy for those who have never felt the stinging darts of segregation to say, 'Wait.' But when you have seen vicious mobs lynch your mothers and fathers at will and drown your sisters and brothers at whim; when you have seen hate filled policemen curse, kick and even kill your black brothers and sisters; when you see the vast majority of your twenty million Negro brothers smothering in an airtight cage of poverty in the midst of an affluent society; when you suddenly find your tongue twisted and your speech stammering as you seek to explain to your six year old daughter why she can't go to the public amusement park that has just been advertised on television, and see tears welling up in her eyes when she is told that Funtown is closed to colored children, and see ominous clouds of inferiority beginning to form in her little mental sky, and see her beginning to distort her personality by developing an unconscious bitterness toward white people; when you have to concoct an answer for a five year old son who is asking: 'Daddy, why do white people treat colored people so mean?'; when you take a cross country drive and find it necessary to sleep night after night in the uncomfortable corners of your automobile because no motel will accept you; when you are humiliated day in and day out by nagging signs reading 'white' and 'colored'; when your first name becomes 'nigger,' your middle name becomes 'boy' (however old you are) and your last name becomes 'John,' and your wife and mother are never given the respected title 'Mrs.'; when you are harried by day and haunted by night by the fact that you are a Negro, living constantly at tiptoe stance, never quite knowing what to expect next, and are plagued with inner fears and outer resentments; when you are forever fighting a degenerating sense of 'nobodiness' – then you will understand why we find it difficult to wait.

As King was waiting, frustrated, for change, so must the reader wait a full page, held in suspension by those semi-colons, while King lists agony after agony, indignity after indignity, before he alights on his final clause, delivered emphatically with an em dash. The experience of reading the sentence is one of waiting breathless and uncomfortable, which amplifies the force of King's description of the misery of waiting for change. This is mimesis at its finest. And this experience of waiting could be created only with the semicolons, which are doing much more here than just separating items in a list or putting some distance between independent clauses. The semicolon is used to open a window on the lived experience of blacks in America in 1963. It's about the furthest thing from an elitist sentiment that I can think of.

Nonetheless, you could say there is certainly something 'elite' about this passage, even as it argues for equal rights. Martin Luther King spoke and wrote in a way that lets his work seamlessly slot into Western scholarly tradition and norms. In the rest of the 'Letter' and in his writings more generally, he cites the classics of the Western canon – Plato, Aquinas, the Bible, Martin Luther, Abraham Lincoln, Thomas Jefferson, Martin Buber, T. S. Eliot, the Declaration of Independence. His writing is elegant and formal. Although it would be a mistake to chalk up to mere performance King's stylistic choices and his careful cultivation of a distinguished intellectual family tree, it is certainly true that, as a deft rhetorician, King is in full control of the register in which he's writing. The putative audience for his letter, after all, was a group of eight white Southern clergymen. In a sense, everything in the 'Letter', from the invocation of St Augustine to the semicolons, is a coded message that says: 'You can take me seriously; I'm *Dr* King; I know the same things you know.'

I'm hardly the first person to home in on the conventionality of King's register. It gets a mention in a speech that the novelist, essayist, and English teacher David Foster Wallace liked to give to black students whose writing he perceived to be, unlike King's, 'nonstandard'. Wallace gave this speech one-on-one to students he believed would benefit from it. It's long, but here's a taster:

> I don't know whether anybody's told you this or not, but when you're in a college English class you're basically studying a foreign dialect. This dialect is called Standard Written English … In this country, SWE is perceived as the dialect of education and intelligence and power and prestige, and anybody of any race, ethnicity, religion, or gender who wants to succeed in American culture has got to be able to use SWE. This is just How It Is. You can be glad about it or sad about it or deeply pissed off. You can believe it's racist and unfair and decide right here and now to spend every waking minute of your adult life arguing against it, and maybe you should, but I'll tell you something – if you ever want those arguments to get listened to and taken seriously, you're going to have to communicate them in SWE, because

SWE is the dialect our nation uses to talk to itself. African-Americans who've become successful and important in US culture know this; that's why King's and X's and Jackson's speeches are in SWE … and why black judges and politicians and journalists and doctors and teachers communicate professionally in SWE … And [STUDENT'S NAME], you're going to learn to use it too, because I am going to make you.

This speech, Wallace claims, is in the service of being honest and realistic about the way that language is wrapped up in politics and power. Students should be pressed into choosing to learn what Wallace calls SWE – Standard Written English, or Standard White English, as he acknowledges it might as well be called. The reason students should be required to learn SWE is that they will be at an extreme disadvantage in the world if they do not do so. This is how the world is whether you like it or not, Wallace says, ostensibly congratulating himself on his brave truth-telling.

Apparently a few students who were subjected to this speech were offended by it, and one lodged an official complaint with the university. I have some complaints about it, too. Did Wallace pull all his white students into his office for an in-camera chat about how it is that they might be upholding elitist power structures by speaking and writing SWE? Did Wallace call out his colleagues in the academy for failing to find ways to make room for ideas expressed by people who might not know – or might simply choose not to use – the secret-handshake grammar of the powerful? Did he make participation in SWE a choice as fraught with moral and political implications as he made *non*-participation in that dialect? No, the onus is on the black student to choose, not on Wallace or anyone else to use his power and privilege to help remake the world.

Later in the essay, he tells the reader that what must have been offensive to the student who complained about his speech was only that he, a privileged white male, was the one making it. Because of his identity, he says, the student just wasn't able to see the 'logic' of his speech. Nice try, DFW, but what logic? So – your argument is: 'We must use one form of speech, Standard Written English, because that's the form of speech we always use.' I'm not persuaded that 'we are doing this already' is sufficient to justify a claim that 'we *ought* to continue to do this' or 'we *must* continue to do this'. Logic is about uncovering and examining assumptions, not perpetuating them. Maybe there is an intelligent, logical argument to be made for choosing SWE as a shared scholarly and professional dialect – but Wallace didn't bother making it.

What is most infuriating about reading Wallace – more infuriating even than his factual errors and logical hiccups, of which there are many in the 'American Usage' essay* – is that it seems he was equipped to understand, for instance, that language is part of our self-presentation, crucial to our construction and conception of ourselves. He understood better than most people that language, and the choices we make surrounding it, is political, *always*. Yet in his 'pep-talk' to black students, he didn't see it as his job to create a world that would be more open to more possible selves than ones like his own. It's a good thing to make students (and even people who've left their student days far behind) aware that there are context-specific costs

----

* For a taste of some of the problems with Wallace's essay, see the *Language Hat* blog's entry 'David Foster Wallace Demolished', http://languagehat.com/david-foster-wallace-demolished/, accessed 5 August 2018. In addition to the mostly sentence-level problems that *Language Hat* highlights, there are glaring argument-level flaws. Those flaws would require a longish essay to elucidate properly, and this book is not the place. The essay is useful here as an example of a very common and very misguided expectation that users of 'standard' English are exempt from justifying that choice.

and benefits in the choice of one English dialect over another. The problem is that Wallace exempts himself (and everyone who already speaks and writes like he does) from responsibility for his own choice, by pretending it isn't a choice at all.

It's an attitude in keeping with Wallace's self-proclaimed snobbery. He was profoundly a snob – or as he called it, a SNOOT,* an acronym Wallace's family used for 'somebody who knows what dysphemism means and doesn't mind letting you know it'. A dysphemism means a derogatory term – like *snoot*, for instance – and you shouldn't feel bad if you didn't know that, nor should you feel exceptionally clever if you did and you got the joke. Each of Wallace's sentences is a stunt of some kind, every clause an Odyssean convolution. For him, being a SNOOT was something to brag about, and it's crucial to his literary style. When I look back on my own snob days, I feel it's something to be embarrassed about. Where Wallace sees moral high ground lush with the fruits of knowledge, I see a desolate valley, in which the pleasures of speaking 'properly' and following rules have choked out the very basic ethical principle of giving a shit about what other people have to say.

---

* '*Sprachgefühl* Necessitates Our Ongoing Tendance'.

Wallace cared a lot about language and punctuation, and I have no problem with that. I love that at his book readings, he read his punctuation aloud along with the words, because he put those punctuation marks in his writing for a reason. His enthusiasm for punctuation and for language more broadly is not the problem, and I don't doubt that he took his role as a teacher of young people seriously. What is problematic to me is the direction in which he chose to channel those interests and concerns: he narrowed the conversation about the politics of language rather than expanding it, by making it one-sided and doing what everyone always does – obligating people who aren't participating in the status quo to step it up rather than asking the people enforcing the status quo to think about, and justify, their own standards and values.

So what happens now, if you're ready to entertain the notion that having plum-picking contests and SNOOTing around isn't the most admirable way to behave? What's left, if we aren't supposed to show our respect and love for language by respecting and loving rules?

Conclusion

AGAINST THE RULES?

It'll be clear to you by now that I disagree with the rule-mongering of the David Foster Wallace types, and the semicolon hatred of Professor Paul Robinson, the guy who feels 'morally compromised' when his little finger plunks the semicolon key. The history of punctuation shows that rules can't be taken for granted as necessary elements of language. For a start, when we consider rules, we have to ask: *whose* rules? Exactly which collection of rules are we supposed to rely upon and remember, when the fortunes of rule systems have depended on their contradicting one another? For over two centuries, grammar books have preached the gospel of rules, and now, when I talk to friends, students, and colleagues about grammar, they lower their voices confidentially to confess sins: *I just don't ever use the semicolon, because I'm afraid I'll do it wrong. I sometimes* want *to use two colons in one sentence, but I'm not* allowed. *I am very confused about the Oxford comma.* Occasionally I've been pulled aside after a talk on the semicolon to be told a story about a dogmatic elementary school English teacher still perched on the now-adult student's shoulder, looking down, judging, even after decades. At times I've felt less like a punctuation theorist than like a punctuation therapist.

Fear, worry, confusion – even if we did manage to agree on one set of rules to follow, we wouldn't be relieved of our anxieties about punctuation. We still have to worry whether we know the rules and have applied them correctly. We have to worry about situations for which we can't find a rule that seems applicable, and hope that the authorities at *The Oxford Manual of Style* address the oversight immediately. And even if we happen to be very very good at remembering the rules and applying their most obscure precepts, we have to wonder if our assiduous applications of these details will strike the average reader as *mistakes** rather than the markers of precision we hope

---

* This happens with grammar rules of all kinds, not just punctuation. When I worked at Yale, I rode the Metro-North them to be: if rules are not natural features of language, then they depend upon there being shared knowledge in order to bestow on our writing the clarity and precision they promise. Rules have never in human history – and are not now – freed us from the pitfalls and challenges of interpreting other people's words and the anxieties of writing down our own.

In spite of this problem, the bromide that *we need to know rules* is constant even among punctuation reformists, and it's such a deeply entrenched idea that grammar writers rarely (if ever) attempt to justify it. Even the philosopher Theodor Adorno, who wrote a beautiful essay, 'Punctuation Marks', which recovered and built upon the humanist ideal of punctuation as musical, advised that rules have to 'echo in the background' even in moments

---

trains from New York to New Haven regularly, and I would often stop at one of the kiosks near the train to get a gin and tonic for the journey. One night, after an especially exhausting conference in the city, I walked up and ordered 'two gins and tonic'. The person manning the kiosk was briefly speechless at being confronted with such an idiot as myself who couldn't even order properly. Finally, perhaps after considering the possibility I might be too drunk already to serve, she asked me if I meant 'two gin and tonics'. I opted not to go into the pluralisation rule and said, 'Sure. The gin is just more important to me than the tonic.'

where the author 'suspends' those rules. Adorno, like just about everyone else writing about punctuation, seems to have believed that we always process writing in terms of its conformity to, or conflict with, rules. When a rule is broken, these theorists believe, we hear the breakage, whether we realise it consciously or not.

But if that were true, it sure would be strange that we can read someone like Shakespeare without having our delicate rule-bound constitutions constantly assaulted by 'false syntax', as the early American grammarians called it. Remember those corrections they made to Shakespeare's verse? Perhaps the experience of reading isn't so much a matter of hearing 'rules' and 'not-rules' as it is about immersing ourselves in a text and adjusting to a way of speaking that might be very foreign to us in terms of time period, culture, or genre. That's a pretty extraordinary skill to have built into our brains, and I'm not sure why we'd *want* to squeeze it out of ourselves by insisting that language is inherently rule-bound.

If rules don't do what they set out to do for us – if rules are just idealisations of language that don't manage either to help us learn to write well, or to describe why a piece of writing is effective or ineffective – does that mean that rules are totally worthless? Not necessarily. In fact, if we can learn to see past rules as the *only* framework with which we can understand and learn to use language, we might be able to see what purposes rules could *really* serve. That is, we can peel away the justification that 'rules are *really in* language' and free ourselves to ask instead: 'What *good* might rules be, even if they aren't strictly *necessary* or *sufficient*?' Rules, considered as frameworks within which to work rather than as boundaries marking the outer limits of rhetorical possibility, might spur creativity, just as a poet might find it productive to work within the strictures of the sonnet form. But we would be making a big mistake to teach that the only 'legal' way to write poetry is to write sonnets. The same goes for punctuation rules.

Perhaps this will be some balm for the souls of some of you who, in spite of the story told in this book, still feel attached to *The Elements of Style* or Fowler or whatever your preferred grammar tome might be. Even if you accept everything I've said in this book about rules, you might still feel, deep down, a love for the idea of grammar rules. But when it comes down to it, I'd wager that the object of your love lies elsewhere. That love is really for the English language, or for orderliness and organisation, or for tradition. None of these things is a foolish thing to love. But if we really love English, or if we love the sense of structure that grammar provides, or if we love traditions and a sense of shared linguistic practices across generations, we have to look somewhere else to celebrate that devotion; rules will be, just as they always have been, inadequate to form a protective fence around English. We will never find *the* rules, unshiftable, unchangeable, and incorruptible. There are no such things.

It's worth thinking carefully about the ethical costs of trying to build that fence anyway. A fence keeps things out as surely as it keeps things in. Who is kept out of our conversations, our public life, and our academies by these language-fences? Rules can be an easy, lazy way to put the onus on someone else: if you make a grammar mistake while trying to convey something heartfelt, I can just point out you've used a comma splice and I'm excused from confronting what you were saying, since you didn't say it properly. What if we thought less about rules and more about communication, and considered it our obligation to one another to try to figure out what is really being communicated? Does it truly matter if there's a grammar error in the email from your intern, or on the sandwich board outside the deli that a new immigrant couple has opened, or in a world leader's tweet?* I care a lot more

---

* Fuck-ups can be fun, but it matters who we're laughing at. If you want to, feel free to print a giant poster-size copy of the previous sentence and have a good giggle at this author with

about whether the President's tweets show the values of democracy versus hatred than I do about where he put a comma. During the 2012 elections, when Mitt Romney ran aggressive campaigns misconstruing President Obama's statements on entrepreneurship, American television host Jon Stewart capped off an indictment of Romney's strategy with, 'Mr. Romney, hanging your attack on a person's slight grammatical misstep is what people do in an argument when they're completely fucked and they know they *have* no argument.' Indeed. Or it's what they do when they don't want to be bothered to hear the other side in the first place: a grammar attack is quite simply an *ad hominem* attack that looks more legitimate because it's dressed up in a cap and gown.

Those of you readers who speak English as a first language, like I do, enjoy a remarkable privilege: we speak the most widely spoken language in all the world. This is a wonderful advantage for us; the pre-eminence of English does as much as aeroplanes and the Internet do to make the world small enough that we can skip across its

---

multiple degrees ending a sentence with a preposition. But don't be like Bristol's so-called Banksy of punctuation or Acción Ortográfica Quito and go around marking up people's store billboards to correct grammar mistakes. That makes you a vandal and a mean-spirited pedant.

circumference in ways both real and virtual that our grandparents wouldn't have dreamed possible. At the same time, many native English speakers never experience what it's like to struggle to communicate basic needs to a shop assistant; or to be lost on the underground, the air filled with indecipherable phonemes that offer no aid; or to be talked down to as though you're an idiot by someone who has heard your foreign accent. Having lived abroad myself, I can recall with yesterday's clarity the casual callousness of a German pharmacist who pretended for five long minutes that she didn't know I was asking for ibuprofen at the Berlin Hauptbahnhof Apotheke because I said '*ich mochte*' (I liked) instead of '*ich möchte*' (I would like); and I can recall with equal clarity the generosity and hospitality of a group of Germans who took the time to have a slow conversation with me in their language while waiting for the TXL bus to come.* I know which type of

---

* I lived in Berlin on and off between 2007 and 2013. When I go back to visit now, even though I'm rusty from lack of practice, I find Berliners are *much* keener to speak German with me, now that their city has been occupied by hordes of British and American expats, many of whom don't bother to learn a single word of German since they can sail along fine speaking English. Perhaps that's made Berliners look at German learners in a new and more forgiving light.

memory I'd rather be in the mind of a tourist, immigrant, Internet forum poster, or any other English-language learner. Having a more advanced knowledge of a language provides a wonderful opportunity to be welcoming and constructive, if you prioritise communication over a set of fictitious rules.

What about that semicolon I argued over with my dissertation adviser so many years ago – the semicolon that launched my deep dive into the history of punctuation and led to this book? Looking back on it now, I was right that it was 'legal'. Semicolons like the one I deployed are shown in the example sentences for *Chicago Manual of Style* rule 6.54, which treats sentences that use elision. But even though it was legal, it was a bad semicolon. What my adviser, Bob, was reacting to (although he'll fight me on this, I'm sure!) was not a lack of rule-following, but the poor rhythm of the sentence, which his practised ear detected and rejected. That's the case with so many instances of grammar-rule violations. When your teacher told you that you can't write a one-sentence paragraph, what he or she really meant was 'I needed more evidence here' or 'This wasn't the right spot in this essay for drama.' Great writers use one-sentence paragraphs all the time, but it is true that they don't always work. It might be more efficient to make a rule against writing a one-sentence paragraph than it is to explain why some particular one-sentence paragraph didn't work, but it's misleading.

Even if they aren't the basis by which we read and write, punctuation rules can't just be unthought as though they never existed in the first place. We could not (and perhaps would not *want* to) go back to a time before there were punctuation rules. But maybe we can think *beyond* them now, to develop a new, more functional, more ethical philosophy of punctuation: one that would support a richer way of learning, teaching, using, and loving language.

ACKNOWLEDGEMENTS

Although brief in length, this book has been long in the making, and countless people have been essential in bringing it to its final full stop.

Robert J. Richards and Lorraine Daston have been the very best and most generous mentors anyone interested in ideas could have. I'm immensely grateful that they encouraged me to think creatively and to take risks, and for the constancy of their confidence in me.

Adrian Johns at the University of Chicago and Françoise Waquet at the Centre national de recherche scientifique in Paris were early advocates for this project, and gamely lent me snippets of their vast expertise in books, language, and the history of the transmission of knowledge. I hope they are reading this book – but not too closely.

My agent, Danielle Svetcov, is an absolute dream. In a literary utopia, all the agents would be clones of Danielle. She's worked tirelessly at all hours of the day and night, fearlessly advocated for me and the book, and either calmed or cultivated my ego depending on what it needed day to day.

The team at 4th Estate, who turned a pile of mere words into this beautiful object, have been magnificent. Anna Kelly, my editor, poured a constant stream of enthusiasm into the book, and showed infinite patience while I crept along, snail-like, with my responses to her incisive editorial guidance. Kate Johnson saved me from myself many times over with her careful copyediting. The book wouldn't have made it across the finish line without Fran Fabriczki and Nicholas Pearson gamely stepping in.

Much of the book was written in a beautiful little carrel in the Senate House Library. My thanks to the library staff, who humoured the sun-starved American who wanted a carrel on whatever side of the library would allow her to absorb maximum light through the little casement windows.

Sundry advice on all manner of things from the aesthetic to the practical was offered generously by Aerin

ACKNOWLEDGEMENTS

Hyun, Leo Vladimirsky, Benjamin Lorr, Ashley Wilson, Tim Casey, Peter Trachtenberg, Liz Gately, and Melissa Wachs. My peers in the Committee on Conceptual and Historical Studies of Science and my colleagues in Language and Thinking were the brightest and most generous first audiences for this project that I could have wished for. Jeff Boggs and Lauren Silvers served up Henry James sources and book cover inspiration; the popovers weren't bad either. Isabel Gabel, co-founder of Rage on the Page, got me through afternoons when I really, really did not want to write. Suzanne Daggett, Nadya Ostroff, Leah Holroyd, and Richard Burgess-Dawson kept me distracted while waiting for auction news. Back in 2012, James Harker told me, 'You know, there could be a *book* in that article'; sometimes you were expecting *ein Glas* but you find out that you've unexpectedly gotten enough for *eine Große Flasche*. David Elkins solved all my MS Word problems while Christian Blood read my footnotes aloud and giggled gratifyingly. Anurag Dhingra, Christina Bloomquist, and Frankie let me borrow their apartment when I needed somewhere to close myself off and write. Marie Regan offered endless encouragement and advice from afar, and she choreographs one hell of a celebratory dance party over Skype. Anjuli Fatima Raza Kolb is my alchemist, always.

I will always owe more than I can convey to the following people: Jason Emery, who has lent me words when I lacked the right ones, and who has endured my roughest drafts without judgment (once you'd seen the one I concealed in an empty yogurt cup, what was left to hide?); Rachel Ponce, who has spent many hours rescuing little things I lost, like all the footnotes to my dissertation (once) and my sense of self-worth (regularly); Niall Mason, who has expanded the boundaries of my worlds both geographical and intellectual; and finally, John Pharis, Sue Ellen Watson, and Parks Watson, fixed stars who have been there from the very beginning and deserve their place here at the most important part of any piece of writing:

The End.

NOTES

INTRODUCTION: LOVE, HATE AND SEMICOLONS

'The semicolon has become so hateful': Paul Robinson, 'The Philosophy of Punctuation', *The New Republic* (26 April 1980). Reprinted 2002 at http://www.press. uchicago.edu/Misc/Chicago/721833.html, accessed 22 October 2018.

ugliness, or irrelevance: Lynne Truss, *Eats, Shoots & Leaves* (New York: Gotham Press, 2003), p. 108.

'representing absolutely nothing': Kurt Vonnegut, *A Man Without a Country* (New York: Seven Stories Press, 2005).

almost 800,000 people: 741.2k shares according to SharedCount.com metrics, using the URLs http://bit. ly/5FNLFV and http://theoatmeal.com/comics/ semicolon. Last verified on 6 September 2018.

'most feared punctuation mark': 'How to Use a Semicolon', *The Oatmeal*, accessed 6 September 2018. http://theoatmeal.com/comics/semicolon

'Pretentious': Robinson, 'On the Philosophy of Punctuation'.

On trendy semicolons: See Chapter Three: 'Sexy Semicolons'.

'purely a species of fashion': George Campbell, *The Philosophy of Rhetoric* (London: W. Strahan, 1776), p. 340.

'gross mistakes': Robert Lowth, *A Short Introduction to English Grammar: With Critical Notes* (London, 1762), p. xii.

'It's tough being a stickler': Truss, *Eats, Shoots & Leaves*, p. 2.

I: DEEP HISTORY

The semicolon was born: On the origins and form of the semicolon, see M. B. Parkes, *Pause and Effect: An Introduction to the History of Punctuation in the West* (Berkeley: University of California Press, 1993), p. 49.

The humanists: Paul Grendler, 'Humanism', *Oxford Bibliographies* (27 June 2017), doi: 10.1093/OBO/9780195399301-0002.

specially cut: Cambridge University Library, 'Pietro Bembo (1470–1547) *De Aetna*', *Manutius and the Bembos* (online exhibition). https://exhibitions.lib.cam.ac.uk/manutius/artifacts/bembo-de-aetna/

sprinkled here and there: Parkes, *Pause and Effect*, p. 49.

'ugly, ugly as a tick': Truss, *Eats, Shoots & Leaves*, p. 108.
'It is not concealed': Quoted in ibid., p. 48.

II: THE SCIENCE OF SEMICOLONS

'something like a complete grammar': Goold Brown, *The Grammar of English Grammars* (1851; New York: W. Wood & Co., 1878), p. i.

'lay down rules': Robert Lowth, *A Short Introduction to English Grammar* (London: A. Millar, 1762), p. xiii.

'few precise rules': Ibid., p. 169.

analogous to the rests: Ibid., p. 172.

English Grammar was a blockbuster success: John A. Nietz, 'Old Secondary School Grammar Textbooks', *English Journal* 54, no. 6 (September 1965): 541–6, http://www.jstor.org/stable/811408

'the best-selling producer': Charles Monaghan, preface to *The Murrays of Murray Hill* (Brooklyn, NY: Urban History Press, 1998), p. vii. Italics mine.

at least *one hundred and ten*: Alma Blount, *An English grammar, for use in high and normal schools and colleges* (New York: H. Holt, 1914), p. 336.

a new system of parsing verbs: F. A. Barbour, 'The History of English Grammar Teaching', *Educational Review* 12 (1896): 492.

extending his predecessors' criticisms: Ibid., p. 497.

'veer his course': Brown, *Grammar of English Grammars*, p. 50.

when Kirkham revised: Ibid., p. 51.

'filled with glad wonder': Ibid., p. 46.

In one particularly efficient passage: Ibid., p. 52.

more boasting: Kirkham in the *Knickerbocker*, quoted in
    ibid., p. 50.

Brown bit back: Ibid.

protests from parents ... and school officials: See, for
    instance, the objections of parents in A. M. Leonard,
    'The Teaching of Grammar: Meeting at the
    Educational Room', *Massachusetts Teacher and Journal of
    Home and School Education* (1 July 1867): 243, and also
    the State of Connecticut's rejection of grammar
    recounted in Barbour, 'History of English Grammar
    Teaching', p. 500.

as early as 1827: 'Philosophical Essays 8', *Masonic Mirror
    and Mechanics' Intelligencer* (24 February 1827): 66.

came to a boil by 1850: Barbour, 'History of English
    Grammar Teaching', p. 498.

persisted through the rest of the nineteenth century: See
    ibid., p. 500; and Charles H. Watson, 'Shifts in
    Educational Methods', *The Watchman* (10 May
    1900):14.

'laws of language': I. J. Morris, preface to *Morris's grammar.
    A philosophical and practical grammar of the English
    language, dialogically and progressively arranged; in which
    every word is parsed according to its use* (New York:
    T. Holman, 1858), p. iii.

'errors' and 'absurdities': Ibid., pp. vi–xv.

eviscerating the stale precepts: Ibid.

'If the truth be disagreeable': Ibid.

championed in the press: G. Dallas Lind, 'Natural Science
in Common Schools', *Massachusetts Teacher* (1 August
1873): 274. Another critic argued that grammar was
important as a science, but that only prior study in
natural science would enable students subsequently to
investigate the fundamentals of English: physics as a
prerequisite for language rules, as it were. See C. A. C.,
'The Natural and Physical Sciences in Our Grammar
and High Schools: A paper read before the Middlesex
County Teachers' Association by C. A. Cole',
Massachusetts Teacher (1 June 1874): 244.

a system of diagrams: Stephen W. Clark, preface to
*A practical grammar: in which words, phrases, and sentences
are classified according to their offices, and their relation to
each other: illustrated by a complete set of diagrams* (New
York: A. S. Barnes, 1847), p. iv.

thought of them that way: See Roberto Torretti,
'Nineteenth Century Geometry', in *The Stanford
Encyclopedia of Philosophy*, ed. Edward N. Zalta, plato.
stanford.edu/archives/sum2010/entries/geometry-
19th/; and Jerome Fellmann, Arthur Getis, and Judith
Getis, *Human Geography: Landscapes of Human Activities*
(Madison, WI, 1997), p. 3.

believed the two disciplines were essential: See 'Subjects
and Means of Instruction', *American Journal of
Education* 10 (March 1861): 141.

'perfect' and 'useful': Anon., 'Teachers and Teachers' Seminaries', *American Annals of Education* 7 [February 1837]: 49.

'leading principles, definitions, and rules': Peter Bullions, *The Principles of English Grammar; comprising the substance of the most approved English grammars extant; with copious exercises in parsing and syntax; a new edition, revised, re-arranged and improved for the use of schools* (New York: Pratt, Oakley, 1859), p. viii.

'in larger type': Ibid.

'to convey to the reader': Ibid., p. 151.

'the duration of the pauses': Ibid., p. 152.

'The foregoing rules': Ibid., p. 155.

'Some may begin to think': Brown, *Grammar of English Grammars*, p. 22.

III: SEXY SEMICOLONS

'Forty-three wore the moustache': 'Beards, Smooth Faces, and So On', *Chicago Daily Tribune*, 16 March 1857, p. 2.

the *un*fashionableness of two other marks: Brown, *Grammar of English Grammars*, p. 773.

'the parenthesis is now': T. O. Churchill, *A New Grammar of the English Language* (London: W. Simpkin and R. Marshall, 1823), p. 362. Quoted in Brown, *Grammar of English Grammars*, p. 773.

'nearly obsolete': Rufus Nutting, *A practical grammar of the English language: accompanied with notes, critical and explanatory* (Montpelier, VT: E. P. Walton, 1826), p. 126; and Bradford Frazee, *An improved grammar of the English language, on the inductive system, etc.* (Philadelphia: Sorin and Ball, 1844), p. 187. Both quoted in Brown, *Grammar of English Grammars*, p. 773.

'little moons': Parkes, *Pause and Effect*, p. 215.

'The COLON is now so seldom used': Oliver C. Felton, *A concise manual of English grammar: arranged on the principle of analysis: containing the first principles and rules, fully illustrated by examples … and a series of parsing lessons in regular gradation from the simplest to the most abstruse* (Salem, MA: W. & S. B. Ives, 1843), p. 140. Quoted in Brown, *Grammar of English Grammars*, p. 773.

'we should not let children use them': 'Punctuation III', *The Common School Journal* (1 February 1850): 42.

'But who cannot perceive': Brown, *Grammar of English Grammars*, p. 773.

'once very fashionable': Ibid.

'The use of the semicolon': H. W. Fowler, *A Dictionary of Modern English Usage* (1926; Hertfordshire: Wordsworth Editions, 1994), p. 568.

mid-century grammarians waffled: Brown, *Grammar of English Grammars*, pp. 770–1. Brown gives a detailed account of the various opinions on punctuation's classification.

four possibilities: G. P. Quackenbos, *An English Grammar* (New York: D. Appleton, 1862), p. 264.

a dependent clause using a semicolon: See, for instance, Brown's *Grammar of English Grammars*, p. 771: 'Of the different kinds of verse, or "the structure of Poetical Composition", some of the old prosodists took little or no notice, because they thought it their chief business, to treat of syllables, and determine the orthoëpy of words.'

grammarians distinguished between rhetorical pauses: See William Chauncey Fowler, *English Grammar* (New York: Harper and Brothers, 1881), p. 743.

still permissible: Ibid., p. 749.

They general prescribed them: See F. A. White, *English Grammar* (London: Kegan Paul, Trench & Company, 1882), p. 212.

'but one use of the semicolon': California State Board of Education, *English Grammar* (Sacramento, CA, 1881), p. 265.

'Where is the man': John Van Ness Standish, 'Too Much Teaching by Rote', *Chicago Daily Tribune*, 24 December 1899.

'From childhood's earliest hour': 'Power of Points: Punctuation That Upset Work of Solons', *Boston Daily Globe*, 20 January 1901, p. 29.

'made trouble in the laws': From the *Indianapolis Journal*, 'A Semicolon Before a Supreme Court: A Legal Treatise on Punctuation or a Changed Method Needed', *New York Times*, 31 December 1895.

The Massachusetts Supreme Court had issued: *David Cushing & another v Paul B. Worrick*, [no number in original], 75 Mass. 382; 1857 Mass. LEXIS 356; 9 Gray 382.

IV: LOOSE WOMEN AND LIQUOR LAWS

'It was an unimportant': 'Saloons Shut by Semicolon', *Chicago Daily Tribune*, 16 December 1900, p. 50.

'The lawyer brushed the dust off': Ibid.

'That no sale of spirituous or intoxicating liquor': Ibid.

'was meant to be and should be construed': Ibid.

the barman's attorney insisted: 'A Semicolon', *Boston Daily Globe*, 6 December 1900, p. 5.

'seemed to take a good bit of enjoyment': Ibid.

'throw light': *Commonwealth v George H. Kelley*; *Same v James Sutcliffe* [no number in original], 177 Mass. 221; 1900 Mass. LEXIS 1038.

'punctuation may be disregarded': *Cushing v Worrick*, 9 Gray 382, paraphrased in ibid.

'The cause of all the trouble': 'Power of Points', p. 29.

'Marks of punctuation may not control': Quoted in ibid.

Police were ordered: 'Saloons Shut by Semicolon', p. 50.

'the proposition before the Senate': 'Semicolon Stays', *Boston Daily Globe*, 11 April 1901, p. 1.

'well known throughout the country': Willard Holcomb, 'Latter-Day Puritans: Boston Not Entirely Devoid of Alcoholic Glee', *Washington Post*, 2 June 1901, p. 19.

'the greatest provoker of profanity': Ibid.

'If every member of this house': 'Semicolon Law
Stays on Books', *Boston Daily Globe*, 7 April 1904,
p. 1.

'friends and foes of the semicolon': 'Liquor Hours: Closing
and Present Law Considered', *Boston Daily Globe*, 8
February 1905, p. 4.

put to a popular vote: 'Plain, Common Sense', *Boston Daily
Globe*, 28 November 1906, p. 6.

The people of Massachusetts approved: 'Hotel Owners
Getting in Line', *Boston Daily Globe*, 13 December
1906, p. 6.

'good sense': Ibid.

'At last': 'Revelry in Boston: The Gorgonian Glare of
Boston Virtue as Cure for the Drink Habit', *New York
Sun*. Reprinted in *Boston Daily Globe*, 15 January 1907,
p. 10.

'members of the association': 'Hotel Men at Banquet
Board', *Boston Daily Globe*, 8 February 1905, p. 4.

V: THE MINUTIAE OF MERCY

'The modern Court': Eig, Larry M. et al., *Statutory
Construction and Interpretation: General principles and
recent trends, statutory structure and legislative drafting
conventions, drafting federal grant statutes, and tracking
current federal legislation and regulations* (Alexandria, VA:
TheCapital.Net, 2010), p. 11.

'true meaning': *United States Nat'l Bank of Oregon v Independent Ins. Agents*, 508 US 439 (1993) at 454. Quoted in Eig et al., *Statutory Construction*, p. 11.

'the Court remains reluctant': Eig et al., *Statutory Construction*, p. 11.

'punctuation is no part of a statute': *Hammock v Loan and Trust Co.*, 105 US 77 (1881) at 84–5.

'punctuation is the most fallible': *Ewing v Burnet*, 36 US 41 (1835).

'punctuation is no part of the English language': *Holmes v Phoenix Ins. Co.*, 9S F. 240. Quoted in *Feliciano v Aquino*, GR No. L-10201 (1957).

a woman gets out of a parking ticket: Sarah Larimer, 'Ohio Appeals Court Ruling is a Victory for Punctuation, Sanity', *Washington Post*, 1 July 2015, accessed 9 September 2018, https://www.washingtonpost.com/news/post-nation/wp/2015/07/01/ohio-appeals-court-ruling-is-a-victory-for-punctuation-sanity/?noredirect=on&utm_term=.e5a5a0c0dd89

'semi-colon which the appellant views': *Feliciano v Aquino*, GR No. L-10201 (1957).

In the early hours: Raymond B. Marcin, 'Punctuation and the Interpretation of Statutes', 9 Conn. L. Rev. 227, 235 (1977).

'We find the defendant': *State v Merra*, 103 N.J.L. 361 (1927).

Alexander Simpson argued: 'Semicolon Plea Fails to Save Murderer', *New York Times*, 17 May 1927, p. 24.

In his dissenting opinion: *State v Merra*, 103 N.J.L. 361 (1927).

'It does not appear': Ibid.

finally making its way to the summer residence: 'Hope Fading for Convicted Slayer', *Boston Daily Globe*, 2 August 1927, p. 5.

Merra went to the electric chair: 'Merra is Executed; Says "I Die Innocent",' *New York Times*, 6 August 1927, p. 28.

'unusually large': 'Bridegroom is Executed 80 Hours After Wedding', *Atlanta Constitution*, 6 August 1927, p. 18.

'What more can two immigrants from Italy expect?': Eric Foner, 'Sacco and Vanzetti', *The Nation* (20 August 1977): 137.

anti-Irish sentiment: W. H. A. Williams, *Irishman's Dream: The Image of Ireland and the Irish in American Popular Song Lyrics, 1800–1920* (Urbana: University of Illinois Press, 1996), p. 148.

forms the climax: Act IV, Scene 1.

VI: CARVING SEMICOLONS IN STONE

'Rules and regulations': *Manual of style, being a compilation of the typographical rules in force at the University of Chicago press, to which are appended specimens of types in use* (Chicago: University of Chicago Press, 1906), p. v.

nineteen regulations: Ibid.

'what everybody else calls it': *The Chicago manual of style: for authors, editors, and copywriters* (Chicago: University of Chicago Press, 1982), p. vii.

'much more a "how-to" book': Ibid.

'the subjective element': Ibid., p. 132.

'recommend a single rule': Russell David Harper, preface to *The Chicago Manual of Style*, 16th edition (Chicago: University of Chicago Press, 2010).

'extrapolate': 'Numbers', *The Chicago Manual of Style Online*, accessed 4 September 2018, https://www.chicagomanualofstyle.org/qanda/data/faq/topics/Numbers/faq0008.html. See also 'Citation, Documentation of Sources,' *The Chicago Manual of Style Online*, accessed 4 September 2018. https://www.chicagomanualofstyle.org/qanda/data/faq/topics/Documentation/faq0028.html

'logical application': *The Chicago Manual of Style*, 17th edition (Chicago: University of Chicago Press, 2017), p. 364.

Turkish and Arabic: Harun Küçük, reply to the author's Facebook post, 16 September 2017.

'the California stop': Paul Festa, Skype call with the author, 18 February 2018.

'in Texas': Tim Casey, reply to the author's Facebook post, 16 September 2017.

VII: SEMICOLON SAVANTS

a 'golly' or two: Mark Twain, *Mark Twain's Library of Humor*, ed. Washington Irving (New York: Random House, 2010), p. 175.

'The damned half-developed foetus!': Shaun Usher, *Letters of Note* (Edinburgh: Canongate Unbound, 2013), p. 206.

'printer's proof-reader was improving': Mark Twain, *Autobiography of Mark Twain, Volume 1: The Complete and Authoritative Edition*, ed. Harriet E. Smith, Benjamin Griffin, Victor Fischer, and Michael Barry Frank (Oakland: University of California Press, 2010), p. 677.

'I use [the semicolon]': Jon Henley, 'The end of the line?' *Guardian*, 3 April 2008, accessed 4 September 2018, https://www.theguardian.com/world/2008/apr/04/france.britishidentity

'Coleridge has chosen': Irving N. Rothman, 'Coleridge on the Semi-colon in *Robinson Crusoe*: Problems in Editing Defoe', *Studies in the Novel* 27, no. 3 (1995): 320–40, http://www.jstor.org/stable/29533073

'I shaved and showered': Raymond Chandler, *The Big Sleep, Farewell, My Lovely, The High Window* (New York: A. A. Knopf, 2002), p. 137.

'would you convey my compliments': Usher, *Letters of Note*, p. 78.

Chandler responded with a poem: Shaun Usher, 'God damn it, I split it so it will stay split', *Letters of Note*

(blog), 20 April 2012, http://www.lettersofnote.
com/2012/04/god-damn-it-i-split-it-so-it-will-stay.
html

'If you can go past': Raymond Chandler, 'Oscar Night in
Hollywood', *The Atlantic* (March 1948), https://www.
theatlantic.com/magazine/archive/1948/03/
oscar-night-in-hollywood/305705/

'I didn't mind what she called me': Raymond Chandler, *The
Big Sleep* (1939; New York: Vintage Books, 1992), p.
158.

The Oxford Manual of Style opines: See https://www.ox.ac.
uk/sites/files/oxford/media_wysiwyg/University%20
of%20Oxford%20Style%20Guide.pdf

'weak-charactered writers': Truss, *Eats, Shoots & Leaves*,
p. 126.

'The sweat wis lashing': Irvine Welsh, *Trainspotting* (New
York: W. W. Norton, 1996), p. 3.

'It wis good fir a while': Irvine Welsh, 'A Soft Touch', *The
Acid House* (New York: W. W. Norton, 1995); reprinted
in Dohra Ahmad, *Rotten English: A Literary Anthology*
(New York: W. W. Norton, 2007), p. 267.

'That bygone time': Rebecca Solnit, 'Diary', *London Review
of Books* 35, no. 16 (2013): 32–3, https://www.lrb.co.uk/
v35/n16/rebecca-solnit/diary

'American men commit murder-suicides': Rebecca Solnit,
Men Explain Things to Me (New York: Haymarket
Books, 2014), p. 24.

'women are capable': Ibid., p. 35.

'Good things came about': Solnit, 'Diary'.

a dramatic chase scene: 'Islands', *Planet Earth II*, BBC Natural History Unit, BBC America, and Zweites Deutsches Fernsehen, 18 February 2017.

three and a half years: Emily Badiozzaman, '27 Mind-Blowing Facts About the Making of *Planet Earth II*', *ShortList* (blog), 12 December 2016, https://www.shortlist.com/entertainment/tv/making-of-planet-earth-ii-david-attenborough-how-they-made/71586

'Remember that writing is not typing': Rebecca Solnit, 'How to Be a Writer', *Literary Hub* (blog), 13 September 2016. https://lithub.com/how-to-be-a-writer-10-tips-from-rebecca-solnit/

there were still first-run copies: Philip Hoare, 'What *Moby-Dick* Means to Me', *New Yorker* (3 November 2011), https://www.newyorker.com/books/page-turner/what-moby-dick-means-to-me

'But if there are any of our readers': 'Book Notices', *United States Democratic Review* (Langtree and O'Sullivan, 1852), 30, p. 93.

'The style of his tale': Quoted in Hershel Parker, *Herman Melville: A Biography* (Baltimore: Johns Hopkins University Press, 1996), p. 18.

'And, as for me': Herman Melville, *Moby-Dick: or, The Whale* (1851; New York: Charles Scribner's Sons, 1902), p. 96.

'Finally: It was stated': Ibid., p. 123.

'"Moby-Dick" is not a novel': Hoare, 'What *Moby-Dick* Means to Me'.

'The plot is meagre': *London Britannia*, 8 November 1851.

'wise, funny, and gripping': Robert Crum, 'The 100 Best Novels', *Guardian*, 13 January 2014.

'When instantly, the entire ship careens': Melville, *Moby-Dick*, p. 264.

'In the case of a small Sperm Whale': Ibid., p. 261.

'Its oceanic reach': Hoare, 'What *Moby-Dick* Means to Me'.

'Is it that by its indefiniteness': Melville, *Moby-Dick*, p. 169.

'mystical and well nigh ineffable': Ibid., p. 162.

'horror': Ibid.

'almost despair[ed]': Ibid.

'Mr. Melville grows wilder': Review in *New York Evangelist*, 20 November 1851. Quoted in *Herman Melville: The Contemporary Reviews*, ed. Hershel Parker and Brian Higgins (Cambridge: Cambridge University Press, 2009), p. 379.

'there is something really overwhelming': D. H. Lawrence, *Studies in Classic American Literature* (1923; New York: Cambridge University Press, 2003), vol. 2, p. 142.

'acute periodic exasperation': Edward Jenks, *The Independent Review* (T. F. Unwin, 1905), vol. 6, p. 105.

'cumbrous and difficult': Ibid., p. 109.

'a more difficult book': William Thomas Stead, *The Review of Reviews* (Office of the Review of Reviews, 1905), p. 314.

'unreadable': Ibid., p. 315.

'Life is too short': Ibid.

'the seasoned reader': *The Reader Magazine* (Indianapolis: Bobbs-Merrill, 1905), vol. 5, p. 381.

'Someone has said': 'William James', *The Chautauquan: A Weekly Newsmagazine* (May 1908).

becomes tortured and effortful: For the comparison of these two passages, see Royal A. Gettmann, 'Henry James's Revision of *The American*', *American Literature* 16, no. 4 (1945): 289, doi:10.2307/2920715.

'He glared at her a moment': Henry James, *The Portrait of a Lady* (London: Macmillan & Co., 1881), p. 247.

'His kiss was like white lightning': Henry James, *The Portrait of a Lady* (1908; Hertfordshire: Wordsworth Editions, 1999), p. 499.

'In the revised version': Dominic J. Bazzanella, 'The Conclusion to *The Portrait of a Lady* Re-examined', *American Literature* 41, no. 1 (1969): 55–63, doi:10.2307/2924346. As Bazzanella and others point out, partly this was the fault of reviewers of the 1881 edition, who couldn't accept the ambiguity of James's original ending. Still, James *chose* to bend to those criticisms.

'the reinstatement of the vague': William James, *The Principles of Psychology* (1890; New York: Dover, 1950), p. 254.

'The boundary line of the mental': Ibid., p. 6.

'Use the word "Field"': William James, *Manuscript Lectures*, ed. Frederick Burkhardt and Fredson Bowers

(Cambridge, MA: Harvard University Press, 1988),
   p. 220.

He used 'vague' as a compliment: James, *Principles*, p. 186.

Robinson, 'Philosophy of Punctuation'.

'exotic' and 'transcends the limits': Hans-Johann Glock,
   'Was Wittgenstein an Analytic Philosopher?'
   Metaphilosophy 35 (July 2004): 419.

'*Der Philosoph behandelt*': Ludwig Wittgenstein,
   Philosophische Untersuchungen (Oxford: Basil Blackwell,
   1958), p. 91.

'The philosopher's treatment': Ludwig Wittgenstein,
   Philosophical Investigations, 2nd edition, trans. G. E. M.
   Anscombe (Oxford: Basil Blackwell, 1968), p. 255.

'profound' semicolon: Erich Heller, *The Importance of
   Nietzsche* (Chicago: University of Chicago Press, 1988),
   p. 142.

'As a rule': [Unsigned review], *Blackwood's Magazine* 131
   (March 1882): 374–82; reprinted in Roger Gard, *Henry
   James* (New York: Routledge, 2013), p. 103.

James's very first interview: Preston Lockwood, 'Henry
   James's First Interview', *New York Times*, 21 March
   1915.

Heinrich von Kleist used the dash: '*Er stieß noch dem letzten
   viehischen Mordknecht, der ihren schlanken Leib umfaßt
   hielt, mit dem Griff des Degens ins Gesicht, daß er, mit aus
   dem Mund vorquellendem Blut, zurücktaumelte; bot dann
   der Dame, unter einer verbindlichen, französischen Anrede
   den Arm, und führte sie, die von allen solchen Auftritten*

*sprachlos war, in den anderen, von der Flamme noch nicht
ergriffenen, Flügel des Palastes, wo sie auch völlig bewußtlos
niedersank. Hier – traf er, da bald darauf ihre erschrockenen
Frauen erschienen, Anstalten, einen Arzt zu rufen;
versicherte, indem er sich den Hut aufsetzte, daß sie sich bald
erholen würde; und kehrte in den Kampf zurück.'* See
Heinrich von Kleist, 'Die Marquise von O',
http://gutenberg.spiegel.de/buch/die-marquise-von-
o-1-580/1

'the dashtard': James Marcus, reply to the author's
Facebook post, 16 September 2017.

'live deep': Henry David Thoreau, *Walden* (1854; New
York: Thomas Y. Crowell, 1910), p. 118.

'In any weather': Ibid., pp. 19–20.

VIII: PERSUASION AND PRETENSION

'pretentious': Robinson, 'Philosophy of Punctuation'.

'favored by writers': June Casagrande, 'A Word, Please:
Writers who use semicolons aren't thinking about the
reader', *Los Angeles Times*, 23 July 2015, http://www.
latimes.com/tn-hbi-et-0723-casagrande-20150723-
story.html

'It seems paradoxical': E. H. Mullin, 'A Plea for the
Semciolon', *The Chap-Book* (1 February 1898), p. 247.

'Perhaps it is easy': Martin Luther King, 'Letter from
Birmingham Jail', www.stanford.edu/group/King/
frequentdocs/birmingham.pdf

'I don't know': David Foster Wallace, *Consider the Lobster*
   (New York: Little, Brown, 2006), Kindle location 1410.
what must have been offensive: Ibid., Kindle location 1542.
a SNOOT: Ibid., Kindle location 922.
he read his punctuation aloud: Andrew Adam Newman,
   'How Should a Book Sound? And What About
   Footnotes?', *New York Times*, 20 January 2006, p. E33.

CONCLUSION: AGAINST THE RULES?

'echo in the background': Theodor W. Adorno,
   'Punctuation Marks', trans. Shierry Weber Nicholsen,
   Antioch Review 48 (Summer 1990): 305.
'Mr. Romney': Carol Hartsell, 'Jon Stewart Slams
   You-Didn't-Build-That-Gate in Romney, Fox News'
   Faces', *Huffington Post*, 26 July 2012, https://www.
   huffingtonpost.com/2012/07/26/jon-stewart-you-
   didnt-build-that_n_1705264.html. Italics mine.

INDEX